PRACTICALLY POSITIVE

PRACTICES FOR CREATING A THRIVING ORGANIZATION

RICH SMALLING

ISBN 978-1-954020-08-5 (Paperback)
ISBN 13: 978-1-954020-13-9 (Ebook)

14 15 16 17 18 19 10 9 8 7 6 5 4 3 2 1

First Edition

This book is dedicated to all leaders seeking to create thriving organizations, and to my dad, who inspired me to take on this project.

TABLE OF CONTENTS

ABOUT THE AUTHOR

BY KENNETH D. SMALLING

R ich Smalling is the fourth of my six sons. While I never told him this, I secretly thought of him as the in-between kid. My young wife and I had three sons in quick succession, right after we were married. There was a gap of three years before Rich came along and another three years before we had twin boys. Even devout Catholics can have their faith challenged by six boys, and when God gave us twins, we took it as a clear sign from above that we shouldn't try anymore for a girl.

Rich was the only one of the boys who heeded my unrelenting advice to get an engineering degree. I was the first in my family to go to college, and I was so proud to get my degree in electrical engineering from the University of Delaware in 1950. Thirty-five years later, I found myself in a packed Cassell Coliseum at Virginia Tech, watching my son receive his degree in chemical engineering. I think my dad would have been proud of me if he had lived long enough to see me graduate. I know that I was immensely proud of Rich, and I was so thankful that we were there to see him graduate.

Throughout his life he has seemed to find himself in the right place at the right time. He works hard and he's no dummy, so maybe he put himself in position to be lucky. I was often stunned by how he seemed to walk right into opportunities. He accepted the only job offer he had after Virginia Tech and moved to West Virginia to work in a chemical plant. Being born and raised on Long Island, his move to West Virginia to work in a chemical plant didn't seem like a stroke of luck at the time. In just a few years, though, Rich was asked to help launch a product line in Europe and moved to France, despite not speaking a word of French. In a year, he moved to a larger facility in the south of Holland, despite only knowing a few swear words in Dutch. The money he saved during his time in Europe helped him pay his way to a master's degree in business from the University of Michigan.

His next stroke of luck was to be the biggest of his life. After business school, he took a job in Philadelphia, where he met his future wife, Anne. As soon as we met her, we understood that she was clearly the best thing to ever happen to him. Thankfully, he listened to our silent prayers and they were married shortly thereafter. A few years later, our prayers were answered again when they had two girls in quick succession—God truly moves in mysterious ways.

Luck just kept coming his way. Rich had been doing internal consulting for his employer in Philadelphia and used those skills to help his wife's family assess the potential acquisition of a struggling business in Austin, Texas. The deal went through and, to his great surprise, Rich ended up leading an organization at the ripe age of thirty-one. American

Innovations (AI) had ten employees and almost no sales in 1995. Its technology was aimed at reading residential electric meters automatically. Ironically, I spent my entire career working for electric utilities, and now he was coming to me for advice. While his father-in-law and I were happy to help him with general market and business knowledge, we were both careful to let him make his own mistakes. And he made his fair share of mistakes. By 1999, AI had stabilized the technology and it had grown, but he and the board realized that AI would never be successful in automatic metering.

That could have been the end of that story. But the investors were patient, and the team at AI was working on a new product line using newfangled things called the internet and the cellular telephone network. By another stroke of luck, AI found new life in the oil and gas industry; another business owned by the same shareholders had identified a need that seemed like a great fit for AI's new products. They went after this need and established a foothold in the oil and gas market. Unfortunately, that foothold wasn't strong enough, and AI was again on the verge of failing in 2003.

Luck showed up again in the form of an unexpected phone call that Rich took in the taxi line outside of the Las Vegas Convention Center. AI had been trying for years to partner with another business that had complementary technology. After being rebuffed many times by this potential partner, Rich learned that business was now for sale. He and his team entered a competitive bid process and ended up acquiring Bass-Trigon Software in March 2003. This acquisition saved AI and provided the missing ingredients for a stable and growing business. Over the next seventeen years, AI completed seven more acquisitions and added many new solutions for its clients.

Throughout his career leading AI, Rich was surprised at how much of his time was devoted to people. He hadn't prepared himself for this in business school, and he had not had many opportunities to lead people until he took over AI. He became fascinated by the challenge of creating an organization that engaged its team members, customers, suppliers, and communities, as well as its shareholders. He became a parent shortly after becoming the leader of AI and saw many of the same learning opportunities at home as he did at work. He joined Young Entrepreneurs Organization and Young Presidents Organization, where he was exposed to many more leaders and stories of their journeys as business leaders. He read everything he could about leadership and made many notes of the things that struck him as good ideas. His owners gave him incredible freedom to experiment with organizational structure.

One day, a fundraiser from the University of Michigan found her way from Ann Arbor to Austin. In that first meeting, Rich was connected to the Center for Positive Organizations at the Ross School of Business. The Center's founders were some of the world's most experienced researchers in Positive Organizational Science, and Rich found a wealth of data that aligned with his experiences as a leader. The marriage of theory and practice over twenty-five years led to this book.

While I'm proud of Rich for what he's done at AI, I'm most proud of him as a father and husband. His daughters were wonderful children and have grown into amazing young women. His partnership with Anne has made him a better person, and I know their union will stand the test of time. I should know about that, since I was married to my lovely Carolyn for fifty-plus years.

A few last things about my son. He was always a crappy liar, so you can probably believe what you're about to read. He always speaks his mind, so I think you'll see he's not holding anything back. He has always been a bit of a smart aleck, so I'd expect a few chuckles along the way. Happy reading.

AUTHOR'S NOTE

My dad died in August 2019, before I started to write this book. When my editor suggested that I include a short a biographical note, I couldn't think of a better way to write one than using my words to voice what I would imagine would be his perspective if he were here today. I'd like to imagine that my dad would have written much of the foregoing if he'd had the chance. He helped give me the courage to tackle this challenge by being the author of five technical books about electric distribution systems.

My use of pronouns in this book needs some explanation. Being a servant leader, my use of first-person singular is limited; the actions and accomplishments of AI or any organization that I was part of are a team effort, so when I use "I" it usually means I'm taking the blame for something. "We" mostly means our team at American Innovations. Since I'm related to the owners of AI and because the owners are a big part of our accomplishments, sometimes "we" includes our shareholders, too.

While I spent twenty-five years leading AI, my experiences also draw upon the many entrepreneurs and leaders I encountered at Young Presidents Organization (YPO) and Young Entrepreneurs Organization (YEO); I am eternally thankful for the many great leaders that I've had the privilege to learn from through my involvement in those organizations. I've also learned a lot from the other businesses that our shareholders have been involved with, especially PGI International, Windsor Foods, Ninth House, Quality Sausage, rateGenius, and Igasamex. The leaders of those organizations were a source of ideas and inspiration. I've also drawn on my leadership opportunities at YEO, Creative Action, the Center for Positive Organizations, Virginia Tech, the Austin Together Fund, and Origin Materials. I have certainly benefited from those opportunities more than I have given to those organizations.

PREFACE

INTERGENERATIONAL MEMO

To: *Younger Me*

From: *Older and Wiser Me*

Re: *Creating a thriving organization*

Listen up! I need to tell you some things I wish I knew when I was your age. As Mom would say about Brussels sprouts, "It's for your own good." I hope that you listen to Older Me better than you listened to Mom.

You think you know about business and leadership. Lord knows you've had plenty of lessons about how not to lead, and not as many examples about how to lead well. I'm here to tell you that you don't know what you need to know yet.

What's inside is the product of many painful lessons that I hope you can avoid. I have no doubt that you will make mistakes of your own. If you're not making any mistakes, you're not reaching for enough. I just want you to make better mistakes than I did and move your organization along farther, faster, and with more joy.

I know you pretty well. In fact, I can safely say that I know you better than you know yourself (right now). You're a great listener and you always have been—when it comes to facts, not so much when it comes to advice. I beg you to listen carefully to the advice and lessons of those who came before you. When you push back on their views, do it gently and with respect, so they will continue to offer their perspectives—and so you won't feel so foolish when you look back and realize how often they were right.

You thought an MBA qualified you as an expert in business. You will soon find out that a psychology degree might have been more useful, because you will be spending a lot of your time with people who are not like you. You will need to understand them, respect them, and motivate them to be better than they thought they could be. You'll eventually realize that no one person can beat a motivated team.

You have no formal training in how to build a culture that engages people. You missed an important opportunity to learn from experienced pioneers in Positive Organizational Scholarship during your time at the University of Michigan. Instead, like many others, you avoided the Organizational Behavior department in favor of the sexier Strategy, Marketing, and Finance courses. Those classes were fine, but it took us years to figure out practical ways to create the conditions for a thriving organization.

You have a lot of catching up to do, but you can do it. I've left you notes from some of the thought leaders that inspired us and some examples to get you started. The ideas in here worked out pretty well in the real world with real people.

Good luck and Godspeed. I know that you will go farther and faster than I did at your age.

INTRODUCTION

I'm absolutely certain that I'm not the only person who wants to go back in time and have a little chat with my younger self. In fact, I'm betting that Adam wrote a few lines to himself about apples, Eve, and Cain and Abel. Doesn't everyone want to do life all over again, knowing what they know now?

I learned a lot in twenty-five years of leading an organization through the twists and turns from start-up to stability. There were a lot of painful lessons that I could not have imagined when I started. There was a lot of joy and inspiration from surprising places. It's no surprise that I look back and wish that I knew as much then as I do now.

When I started my leadership journey, I read plenty of stories about great business successes and spectacular failures. Those stories were often digital: either a one or a zero—either you won or you lost. There wasn't a lot I read about *good* businesses and leaders. You were on the cover of a magazine or newspaper either for something really good or really bad. What I realize now is that you never hear anything about a majority of businesses, and a lot of those are doing some really great things.

When I got the chance to lead a business, I didn't think about creating a thriving organization. I was young and I thought mostly about success in terms of profit and growth. I didn't think much about how I would become a good leader. I thought if I did what I did as an employee, people would follow me. I didn't realize that I would be spending most of my time working on people. I thought it would be easy. I was sure I could do better than a lot of the management I was exposed to along the way.

I realized pretty quickly that I didn't know much about leadership. I went to a very good business school, and most of us focused on business—not leadership, not people, not society. That may sound surprising and maybe even disconcerting. Back then, I thought I was going to school to learn about running a business, not about how to create and lead an organization on a meaningful mission and toward worthwhile goals.

Ironically, after spending many years teaching myself and learning a lot of hard lessons, I found that the business school I attended had some of the foremost experts on leadership and thriving organizations. If only I had recognized that business is about people, and leadership is about corporate strategy, finance, and marketing! I would have had the opportunity to learn, as today's students do, how to create an engaged and happy group of people and satisfy all of the stakeholders in a business, including its shareholders.

Looking back on the hard lessons I learned, there are

many things I wish I could tell my younger self. This book is a reflection on the positive practices that we eventually implemented in the real world. Many of these ideas are borrowed from others. Often practices were adapted to our specific situation. Some of our ideas are backed only by instinct, trial and error, hope and prayer. Many are backed by research, good books, and trusted sources.

This book is intended to help you create a thriving organization of people. If you're trying to do that, by my definition, you are a leader. You've assigned yourself the task of looking out for others and being accountable for more than your own actions. As Brené Brown says in her book *Daring Greatly*: "A leader is anyone who holds her- or himself accountable for finding potential in people and processes. [It] has nothing to do with position, status, or number of direct reports."[1] People lead in all kinds of different ways and often without a title. At the most basic level, you are the boss of you, and I hope there are things in here that you can apply to leading your own life. As a parent, by my definition, you are a leader of your family. I contend that good management in business has much in common with good parenting. In fact, I see a similar dynamic between business and family: management/parents versus employees/children, working on opposite sides of the table in a zero-sum game. As I wrote this book, I realized that a lot of what we try to do at work is to get people onto the

> This book is intended to help you create a thriving organization of people. If you're trying to do that, by my definition, you are a leader.

same side of the table, solving problems together. That applies to families as well.

You might be starting out in your career, or you might be many years into it. You might have just taken over a department in your first role as a manager. You might be the Executive Director of a nonprofit. Maybe you're a hired gun looking to change the culture of a struggling company. And yes, you might be a parent, in charge of your own little business at home. If you're trying to create a culture that delivers positive results, then I think you might find an idea or two in here to help you and your team. My hope is that these practices will help you, no matter where you are in your leadership journey.

This book is organized into three sections:

1. Foundational Practices
2. Accelerator Practices
3. 1-2-1 Process

There is also an appendix with examples of how we implemented some of these ideas, so you don't have to start with a blank slate. Along the way, I include a few notes to help guide you.

Foundational Practices are the bedrock of a thriving organization. First, let's take a minute to define a thriving organization. Mine is this: a thriving organization is one where all of the stakeholders are elevated because that organization exists. The organization is energizing, engaging, learning, and performing. We live in the real world of human imperfection, so this does not mean the organization is a paradise for everyone all the time. People make mistakes, so the organization makes mistakes. A thriving organization learns from those mistakes, accepts imperfection, embraces its stakeholders, and balances their needs effectively. A company's stakeholders include its customers, employees, suppliers, communities, and shareholders. Most organizations can use the company example as a way of defining their own stakeholders.

Without these foundational practices it will be difficult, if not impossible, to thrive. When I became responsible for an organization, I didn't realize how important these practices were going to be. These days, thankfully, most business schools provide opportunities for students to learn about the importance of these practices. Plenty of books have been written about these ideas, and more companies are adopting them. These are the practices that I want my younger self to implement as soon as possible. Like the foundation of a solid home or a great basic education, these are the basis for infinite potential.

Accelerator Practices are techniques that throw fuel on the fire of thriving organizations. These practices tend to be easier to implement across an organization than the foundational practices. They can relatively quickly accelerate engagement, learning, joy, trust, and respect. They can be deployed even without the foundational practices in place. This is another level of drawing people together to multiply the impact of a group over the individual. This is the warm fire in the hearth at home. This is what helps turn your reliable sedan into a Tesla.

The 1-2-1 Process ("one-to-one") is a systematic process for maintaining your high-performance vehicle. It's a mechanism for ensuring continued alignment, learning, growth, and performance. None of these practices are groundbreaking. However, it took me a long time to discover them, package them up, and practice them with humans in the real world. As a teenage driver, I knew how to put gas in the car and make sure there was windshield washer fluid. I didn't know anything about how to keep the car running at peak performance.

By the way, 1-2-1 is how we chose to brand the process for encouraging a productive one-on-one relationship between individual and manager. That basic connection is probably the single most critical factor in creating a powerful relationship between individual and organization. People more often leave because of their managers, not the company. Employees often look at managers as impediments to be avoided at all costs rather than as coaches, mentors, and accelerators. Children sometimes view parents the same way.

The 1-2-1 Process is focused primarily on the individual, and responsibility for it lies primarily with the individual. Think of it as an athlete's training program; the coach can guide, inspire, and even cajole, but peak performance doesn't happen without the athlete's dedication, passion, and hard work.

The foundation for the 1-2-1 Process was laid quite accidentally in a chance encounter I had with a 1983 article in a research journal.[2] Then we borrowed ideas from others and came up with a few ideas of our own, all around the same time. We decided to package the whole thing under one initiative, so people could see the complete plan. Years later, we continue working to make the entire thing into an organizational habit. We followed good change management practices and implemented the easiest bits first. We took a step, learned, adjusted our approach, and took another step. Much of the 1-2-1 Process has made it into our organizational lingo. We talk about position alignments, not job descriptions; we do reflections, not performance evaluations.

The practices in this book are aimed at bringing management and employees onto the same side of the table as colleagues solving problems together, rather than sitting across from each other in a no-win, zero-sum battle. This is another important theme of this story, and I'm asking Younger Me to pay particular attention to this point.

Younger Me did not understand the dynamics of employee versus management, or the magic that happens when we work as trusted colleagues with shared goals, respect, and compassion. Younger Me was still wrestling with the transition from being an employee to being management.

Becoming "management" helped me see what goes on behind the scenes. Suddenly, I knew the facts behind the workplace rumors. If a colleague colored outside the lines, I knew about it, and most likely I had to help clean up after it. As time went on, I became increasingly surprised and shocked about what people would do in the workplace. After some time, sadly, I become somewhat anesthetized as a coping mechanism. Colleagues are not often exposed to these incidents (by design), and companies are not going to talk about them beyond the bare minimum (also by design), so most employees are blissfully unaware of bad behavior at the expense of the company. If companies posted these things on Glassdoor, there would be a lot more people reading the reviews (and a whole lot of lawyers going after those companies).

After having railed against the stupidity of management during my years as an employee, I was living an entirely different perspective. And, eventually, I dedicated myself to trying to draw people into the business, break down the walls, and work toward building an organization of trusted colleagues.

One of the many things I never considered about leading an organization is that people arrive at the doorstep with baggage, and it often takes a long time to recognize what people have been carrying around for most of their lives. Most have been raised in organizations that have not tried to provide the right conditions to make people feel engaged. Like touching a hot stove, many people have learned from past experience that leaders and companies are not looking out for their interests. Relationships depend on trust, and both sides of the employment relationship don't often start out with a high degree of trust.

What Younger Me needed to hear were more of these stories to understand the problem at hand, and then to learn how to employ a host of tools to repair the relationship. How can we restore the trust in the relationship between company and employee?

Leaders have the opportunity to help people unpack some of their baggage and fill it back up with more positive and constructive memories. As we do so, we also help them become better versions of themselves, at work and at home. Better versions of people, like products and services, generate more satisfied customers, grow sales, and drive profits. And it pays off at home and in our society. Organizations that enable this will receive loyalty beyond monetary rewards and operate with lower costs and risks. And best of all, in the end, people will forever remember thriving organizations and great leaders with a glow that is better than anything money can buy.

I became a parent about the same time that I began to lead an organization. As we walked out of the hospital holding our first child, we were filled with joy, love, and . . . terror. There was no user manual and no test we had to take to certify that we were capable of taking care of this precious life. So, we started reading every parenting book we could find. If you've ever done that, you realize that a lot of them are not very helpful. For every five or ten you pick up, you find one or two with practical help that seems to work in the real world. I found many similarities between parenting and managing a group of people. Many of my early leadership lessons came from parenting books. Great leaders and great parents have many things in common—genuinely caring for those in our care and putting their needs above our own. As I read books on business and leadership, I found many that were just like those parenting books—lots of advice that seemed impractical or impossible to do in the real world. I most valued the ones that I came across that imparted lessons and ideas that worked with real people.

I do *not* intend for this book to be long on marketing and short on practical help. Over 11,000 books about business are published each year.[3] Amazon has 60,000 books about leadership and 100,000 books about parenting.[4] What the world needs now is *not* another love song.

This is not a textbook. I'm not a researcher or an academic. I've quoted authors who influenced my views, and often they've already said it better than I could have. I've cited some research to add credence to my experiences. I've referenced a number of incredibly talented, experienced, and respected practitioners. If you're looking for something steeped in facts and the science behind the practices, I can try to direct you to where you can find more. I hope that everyone that I've (unwittingly) roped into this gig is okay with the liberties I've taken and accepts that I've joined the fight, albeit without buckets of credibility other than gray hair and scars.

It is my hope that the ideas in this book will be actionable and impactful. I will be completely happy if any of these ideas inspire just one leader to do better. I hope that just one idea helps a leader create a little more engagement, makes a group thrive a little bit, and sends a worker home to their family with energy and confidence. Do your part to help business make lives better. Your reward may not be apparent at all. Praise doesn't come easily for most people. You will likely not be in the room when you get your reward as one of the people in your care speaks with love and admiration about the leadership you provided and how you helped make them a better person. *You can be that leader.*

TAKEAWAYS

- This book is intended to provide actionable ideas to help any leader create a more positive and thriving organization.
- A thriving organization is one where all of the stakeholders are better off because that organization exists. A thriving organization learns from mistakes, embraces all of its stakeholders, and balances their needs effectively.
- This book is for leaders and organizations of all kinds. At the most basic level, you can adopt these practices for you alone. At the end of each section, I will try to describe how the practice can apply to you and your family.
- Throughout the book, I hope to provide the perspective of both employee and management in an effort to break down walls and encourage people to consider the organizational baggage they have been carrying around that gets in the way of a thriving organization.
- This book is about helping to get people on the same side of the table looking for win-wins instead of negotiating win-lose. It's about creating a bigger pie, not grabbing a bigger slice.
- This book is divided into three main sections:

1. **Foundational Practices** are the bedrock of thriving organizations. They establish the culture and boundaries. They clearly describe the "why" driving

the organization and its stakeholders. Without these practices, it will be difficult to truly thrive.

2. **Accelerator Practices** are techniques that throw fuel on the fire of thriving organizations. These practices tend to be easier to implement across an organization than the foundational practices.

3. **The 1-2-1 Process** ("one-to-one") is a systematic process for maintaining your high-performance vehicle. It's a mechanism for ensuring continued alignment, learning, growth, and performance.

QUESTIONS AND ACTIONS

- Think about the most inspirational leaders you have had in your life. What practices did they adopt that moved you to be a better version of yourself? What obstacles do you think they encountered in adopting those practices?

- Think about the leaders you've been exposed to that made you angry. What are the top three things you wished they would have learned about good leadership? How have you adapted your own leadership style to avoid their mistakes?

- Were your parents any of the leaders you thought about? Why or why not?

- Write down five things you wish you could tell

your younger self as you entered the working world. How could you express those in terms of positive practices that you wish you would have adopted in your own life?

- Consider the organizational baggage that you have collected in your career. How does it prevent you from engaging with your organization to create a meaningful partnership where you can thrive? What can you unpack and discard to live a more satisfying working life?

- If you are "management," what are you doing to stay connected to the perspective of your employees? If you have not been in management, how can you become more knowledgeable about the perspective of companies and management? How can you help bring together different perspectives to solve interesting problems and make things better?

ESTABLISHING THE BASIS FOR A THRIVING ORGANIZATION

***Older Me** <grayhairandscars@gmail.com>*

To: *Younger Me*

Re: *Eat Your (Organizational) Vegetables*

Hey Young,

Mom used to say, "Eat your vegetables, they'll help you grow big and strong." Funny that she was only about four feet eight inches tall. But boy, she was strong: a real mighty mite. But I digress. I just wanted to tell you to remember what Mom said. Strength requires lasting commitment.

You're going to be impatient. You're going to want a lot of change and you're going to want it fast. You're young though, so it's to be expected. *Roget's Thesaurus* says that "impatient" is a synonym for "young." For many of us, that impatience doesn't wear off as we get older.

Foundational practices require patience and dedication. These are what build a strong and thriving organization. These are the ones you should get cracking on as soon as you can. Some of them are pretty easy to start, but they take sustained effort to take hold. You can't exercise once a week and expect to be in peak condition.

Stick with it. Perfection is not the goal. Consider all of these practices a work in progress. Get started soon, and don't overthink it too much. You don't have to do it exactly the way I did it. In fact, you need to do it your way. Use what

I'm providing as a guideline to avoid the paralysis of facing a blank sheet of paper.

In this section, you'll find out what would cause someone to tattoo your company logo on their body in permanent ink. You'll take inspiration from the fact that the only time you don't have any problems is when you're dead. And you'll get the chance to teach people what good leadership looks like, so you don't have to go through this alone.

You have the power to change your world. You're the leader, and the people are looking for you to move mountains. If you're frustrated because you can't change your city or your country, take heart, because right now you control your organization. Given all the injustice we see in the world that seems intractable, the one thing that inspired us and gave us joy was having the ability to decide how we managed our little town.

You're ready to tackle something transformational; I can see it in your eyes. You're ready for the discipline, courage, and energy to turn significant organizational change into a habit. Time's running out, and the gray hair is coming up in your rearview quickly. Let's get after it and make our little town a thriving place!

With kind regards (and aches and pains),

Older

CHAPTER 1

COMPELLING PURPOSE

Have you ever wanted to tattoo a company's
logo on your body in permanent ink?

Thriving starts with "Why." People cannot thrive if they don't have a meaningful purpose behind what they are doing.

The most amazing job I've ever seen of creating a compelling purpose was by a friend who founded a business that makes banking software. Banking software? How on earth do you make people want to walk over hot coals for banking software?!

It so happens that his customers are small community banks. His software helps those banks compete with the big banks. Following that trail led his team to want to help the little guy stand up to the big guy, like David and

> People cannot thrive if they don't have a meaningful purpose behind what they are doing.

Goliath—our innate desire to root for the underdog. He crafted an entire ethos around the legendary Battle of Thermopylae and its 300 Spartans. Against all odds, a small and courageous group can make a difference.

He went a step further and captured the essence of his values and purpose in a picture—a Roman shield where the quadrants represented his values and the shield tied to the myth of his compelling purpose.

How compelling was this purpose? Before too long, an employee got a tattoo of this picture. On his body. In permanent ink. That led to more tattoos, then a reward for other employees that got one (in a place that he could see without HR present). And that soon led to a policy about tattooing the company logo on your body. And a few uncomfortable exit interviews.

Did I mention his purpose was compelling? What happened next was incredible. A customer got a tattoo. Really. And another, and another. Now, most of us *really* don't want to disappoint our customers. We strive to build a relationship that inspires loyalty. If a customer has a permanent tattoo of your logo on his body, that's upping the ante. This is putting the "cult" in culture. I really don't worry that you'll have to worry about this problem. If you can get in the ballpark and be real, you'll see the benefits.

Once in hand, a compelling purpose will change how everyone sees your business (or your group, or your department, or even you as an individual). Building an entire ethos around your purpose, driving it through your business and culture, and making decisions with this purpose in mind . . . those things will take time. The magic can start right away, once you have that higher purpose on paper.

Daniel Pink's *Drive* is one of the books that Younger Me thankfully picked up and read carefully. It's an important book about motivation, and Younger Me was in desperate need of help there. Younger Me thought about motivation as carrots and sticks. Pink presents a compelling argument for a new and more positive way of thinking about motivation. He accurately articulates that leaders are responsible for creating the right environment for our intrinsic motivation to kick in. Pink quotes psychology professor Edward Deci, "Human beings have an inherent tendency to seek out novelty and challenges, to extend and exercise their capacities, to explore and to learn. This drive is fragile and needs the right environment to survive."[5]

Pink deems the carrot and stick as Motivation 2.0. He cites Deci saying, "When money is used as an external reward for some activities, the subjects lose intrinsic interest for that activity."[6] Carrots and sticks are unpredictable, diminish performance, extinguish creativity, encourage unethical behavior, become addictive, and foster short-term thinking. This all rang true with what Younger Me was experiencing and resulted in a deep distrust of monetary incentives. Autonomy, purpose, and mastery were, in the real world, much more effective than carrots or sticks.

Pink writes that "Where Motivation 2.0 sought compliance, Motivation 3.0 seeks engagement."[7] Engaged colleagues working together make business a much more manageable and joyful experience for everyone. Older Me found that developing a compelling purpose for our business was the most straightforward intrinsic motivation to implement. There are many more ways to deliver autonomy, and it is powerful, though there are also ways that we found it can go sideways. Mastery is an art in and of itself. Coaches who find a way to keep people at the edge of flow, straining just enough to be great without becoming discouraged, are artists. Purpose was easier to tap into at scale. Pink writes:

> The most deeply motivated people—not to mention those who are the most productive and satisfied—hitch their desires to a cause larger than themselves. . . .The aims of these Motivation 3.0 companies are not to chase profit while trying to stay ethical and law-abiding. Their goal is to pursue purpose—and to use profit as the catalyst rather than the objective. . . .In the workplace people are thirsting to learn about how they are doing . . . meaningful information about their work. . . . It's in our nature to seek purpose. But that nature is now being revealed and expressed on a scale that is demographically unprecedented and, until recently, scarcely imaginable. The consequences could rejuvenate our businesses and remake our world.[8]

Bob Quinn and Anjan Thakor present a compelling case for ensuring your business has articulated a higher purpose.[9] Managers who pursue higher purpose invest more capital, take greater risks, and incur lower costs of compensating their employees. The pursuit of a higher purpose generates positive energy in leaders and employees—a sort of off-balance-sheet asset. People who dedicate themselves to the realization of a higher purpose report higher levels of meaning in life and have higher scores on happiness, well-being, life satisfaction, life control, and work engagement; and lower scores on negative affect, depression, anxiety, being a workaholic, suicidal ideation, substance abuse, and the need for therapy.

Sign me up for that!

As they say on those cheesy infomercials, "But wait! There's more!" In pursuing a higher purpose, people will put others' interests ahead of their own, make spontaneous contributions to the whole, put aside their normal baggage about hierarchy, transcend job descriptions, share information, and listen better. An analysis of thirty Fortune 500 companies showed that companies who articulated a higher purpose outperformed the market average by a ratio of 8 to 1.[10] (If you're looking for an authority on the impact of purpose, there's nobody I've met that is more of an expert, nobody more passionate on the subject, and no more inspiring speaker than Bob Quinn.)

Excited about articulating a higher purpose? You bet! Where do you start? Well, sometimes it's a good idea to start the same way I start most home improvement projects: a cold beer. Seriously, this is something you should tackle when you and your team can find a little relaxed time for creativity. It's not something to do at your morning standup or after going through fifty emails. When you think about thinking outside of the box, who do you want by your side? In my experience, a little creative thought from a small team can generate a lot of progress. Start by yourself and see what you can do alone. Then bring in no more than five other people whom you believe can think outside of the box.

What you're trying to do is describe your business in terms of how it benefits the world. Every business is trying to make money and delight the customer. How does your business purpose ignite passion in people? What are you doing to help make the world a better place? How is your group making things better for others? This is not salary and health insurance. This is why you'd get up at 5:00 a.m., drive through a snowstorm, and pull another grueling fourteen-hour day, then drive home exhausted but feeling deeply satisfied.

A little creative thought from a small team can generate a lot of progress.

John Mackey and Raj Sisodia provide great guidance on this in *Conscious Capitalism*. "Great purposes are transcendent, energizing, and inspiring for all the interdependent stakeholders."[11] They list four categories of great purposes:

1. The Good: Service to others, improving health, education, communication, quality of life
2. The True: Discovery and furthering human knowledge
3. The Beautiful: Excellence and the creation of beauty
4. The Heroic: Courage to do what is right to change and improve the world

My banking software friend chose the Heroic purpose—or at least what I would consider a subset of that category about the little guy prevailing against all odds or standing up for what's right. At our company, we went with the Good.

Our company's mission originally was this: "Help prevent the corrosion of buried metal structures through cathodic protection." No, really, that's what it was. Who wouldn't be inspired to come to work with that hanging on the wall? Just tossing that out at a cocktail party ensured an evening free of human contact. A small improvement we made

> How does your business purpose ignite passion in people? What are you doing to help make the world a better place?

was: "We help oil and gas customers comply with regulations by providing reliable solutions." A little better, but not much.

It's not that far of a leap to: "We protect people and the environment by helping our nation's energy infrastructure operate safely and efficiently." But boy is it a leap in terms of how it makes people feel about coming to work. And it's genuine—it's not marketing hype. Running under our feet every day are thousands of miles of steel pipelines carrying stuff that goes boom. Even if it doesn't go boom, it will make a holy mess of most things it comes in contact with.

Those pipelines are essential. Until we figure out a way to create power for everyone that doesn't involve fossil fuels, that's what we've got. It's difficult to convey how much of our energy needs are carried safely under our feet every day. If not for pipelines, our highways would be packed with tanker trucks carrying stuff that goes boom. None of us want to imagine driving on highways like that—even worse, imagine your sons and daughters on those highways.

Our business really does protect people and the

environment. And authenticity must be at the heart of your compelling purpose. People are trained to see marketing whitewash a mile away. If you go

Authenticity must be at the heart of your compelling purpose.

there, you'll be worse off than you were without a compelling purpose. Make it real. If it's authentic, it's a good start. Don't let perfection be the enemy of progress. I only know one person who created a purpose powerful enough to inspire tattoos.

Once you think you've got the handle on this, bring in more people. Talk with your colleagues to understand why they work with your organization. Talk with your customers about the value you deliver. Think about your community and your suppliers. What inspires all of your stakeholders? This might feel like panning for gold. You might have to sift through a lot of comments for a few worthwhile nuggets. Use them to build on your concept.

Maybe you're thinking: *My business is really boring. It's worse than cathodic protection of buried metal structures. I really don't think there's a good way to put an authentic smear of lipstick on this pig.* Okay, first of all, I feel sorry for you, because it must be tough to go to work every day. But second, there's hope. It may take two cold beers, but you can get there. Keep digging around for the "why" that makes people want to be around your organization. Somehow, someway, your organization makes life better for its stakeholders.

Like many companies, we hold an annual customer meeting. As the CEO, I usually gave a short opening talk to kick off the meeting. Shortly after we established our current purpose statement, I decided to describe what it means to us and how we take our jobs seriously, because our customers are entrusted with an important job—they stand between all of us and disaster. If they don't do their jobs well, things go boom, people can die, and environmental damage can be extensive.

As I spoke, I looked out at the audience. A lot of our customers work in the field. They drive pickups and wear work boots. They are not management or corporate. They are often gruff and cynical. Front and center during my talk was a gentleman slouched in his seat, sipping coffee and looking decidedly uninterested. His posture said, "This is better than being at work, but not by much."

I kept glancing at this gentleman throughout much of my short talk. As I related how important his role is, he literally sat up straighter in his seat and really focused on what I was saying for the first time. I'm sure it wasn't just the coffee kicking in. Afterward, my first thought was how powerful a compelling purpose can be. My second thought was how sad it was that his own company never pointed out to him how important his job is.

He thought he was monitoring cathodic protection systems. It turns out that he was doing his part to protect people and the environment from disaster. Think for a moment about the ripple effect of that reframing. One day he's just driving a pickup truck for some big nameless corporation so he can pay the rent. The next day he's a valued hero fighting to safely deliver the energy we need. In which case is he more engaged and prouder of the work he's doing? Does he come home with a different attitude under those scenarios?

You may be saying to yourself, "You're not running the show, and you're not going to be able to create a higher purpose for the entire organization. Maybe there's something easier in this book that I can try." Don't touch that dial yet! Purpose applies to a group of any size.

> There are 3 major things that hold a team together: purpose, trust, and ownership. . . . Any good team must center on something larger than itself. . . . Whenever you can create an environment of shared success, it helps people find purpose and feel relied upon by others. The social connection ignites a desire to contribute while not letting others down.[12]

There are two important points in that quote by Robbins. First, "Centering on something larger than ourselves" translates to a group that is humble, cooperative, and giving. As soon as we all start thinking about what's in it for ourselves, and that alone, as humans, we give up the advantages we gain from working as a group. This is borne out in the research I cited from Bob Quinn; we stop sharing and caring about each other, and we devolve into selfish combat. Higher purpose unites us and allows us to be better than we can be alone.

Higher purpose unites us and allows us to be better than we can be alone.

The second highlight from the quote by Robbins is "Igniting a desire to contribute while not letting others down is critical to achieving goals." Sticks and carrots are no match for the motivation of not wanting to let people down whom we care about. I once set a goal to do what for me was a very difficult bike ride. Halfway up, I wanted to quit. Three quarters of the way through, I wanted to curl up in a ball and die. But I persevered. Why? Because I announced my goal to my daughters, and I would die before I went back and told them that I quit because it was too hard.

This is another reason why it's good to connect our colleagues to the people who work for our customers and not just the company. Our people develop relationships with people, not ExxonMobil. We know who pays the bills, and we really want that carrot. But if we know Jane Smith at Exxon and we see her face when we think about Exxon, our people will run through brick walls to keep from disappointing her. And if you know that, you'll be that Jane Smith for your own suppliers, too.

All of this works whether you are talking about the company or a group or your family. You can create the power of purpose by thinking about what your team does for the organization that is motivational. Maybe the administrative team's purpose is "We take care of all the stuff that gets in between the business and its stakeholders, the pipes and wires running through the walls in our house that we all take for granted every day, until something goes wrong. We don't make money for the organization, we spend it, so we need to do so wisely, and we need to care about our internal customers like we do about our biggest external ones." Imagine how it would feel if IT contacted you before you started work to find out what kind of computer you wanted and what software you wanted loaded onto it. Imagine if that machine was ready for you on day one and a support technician kindly walked you through the setup and answered your questions promptly and respectfully.

Bringing it Home

You can create the magic of purpose in your family. For Younger Me, my purpose was to leave home as soon as possible before my older brothers killed me and so I could have some freedom.

There is a meaningful "why" in you and your organization.

What if your family's purpose is to ensure everyone gets the lifelong gift of education, learns the value of money, and commits to giving back to the community in a meaningful way? Does that intentional message change the conversation around the dinner table? Does it make leading your own "company" at home a more manageable and joyful experience?

Purpose is the answer to why you exist. It's the meaning of your organizational life. If your only purpose is to make money, then everyone involved in the endeavor will make decisions through that lens. Have you ever been involved with anyone or anything where the primary reason for being is money? That's not what I would describe as a thriving environment. There is a meaningful "why" in you and your organization. Tapping into that creates a magical foundation for things to come.

TAKEAWAYS

- An organization of people cannot thrive without a meaningful purpose. The leader needs to ensure that all stakeholders know the essential value delivered by the organization.

- There is a great deal of research about the many benefits of a clear and compelling purpose, including higher engagement, better financial results, and healthier team members.

- I witnessed this myself after our company turned its staid mission statement into a clear description of the value we helped bring to society through our products and services.

- Purpose works, no matter the size of the organization. You can establish a meaningful purpose for your own group or department by describing the service you provide to others.

- A meaningful purpose is an essential ingredient for living a meaningful life.

QUESTIONS AND ACTIONS

- Has your company articulated a clear and compelling purpose? If so, what impact has it had on you, compared with other jobs you've had that didn't make that connection for you?

- Does your family have a purpose? If not, what do you think it should be? Do you think the many proven benefits of purpose would apply to your family?

- What is your own purpose statement? What would be the impact on your life if it was guided by a clear and compelling purpose?

CHAPTER 2

AUTHENTIC VALUES

*People can't build the culture you want until you
tell them what that looks like and how to live it.*

There's a story we tell about what our value of Relentless
means. In one part of our business, professional certifications demonstrate a depth of knowledge that customers
will pay more for to access. These certifications are difficult
to achieve. The highest level requires weeks of preparation,
and all levels require both classroom testing and practical
demonstration of techniques in the laboratory and in the field.
Colleagues who achieve these certifications make more money
and solve more interesting customer problems.

One of our team members, whom I'll call Joe, failed his
certification test twice. We pay the cost of taking the test the
first time, and we pay half the cost for the second attempt.
Any further attempts are on the employee's dime. The cost of
the test is about a week's pay for these employees. That cost is

on top of the weeks of preparation for the test. After the second attempt, Joe gave up. For years afterward he was reliable, yet uninspired. Over time, his performance declined. Despite discussions and action plans, things weren't getting better. Just as his manager was going to let him go, Joe showed up at his door. "I really want to take the test again. If you'll help me, I think I can do it," he said.

For the next seven weeks, his manager and two other colleagues came into work on Saturdays to help him prepare for the test. The other colleagues were making their first attempt. They seemed to pick up the material a little quicker than Joe, who struggled with the practical tests. Everyone pitched in to help, spending extra time after class to ensure that they were all ready to go. Finally, the test day arrived. When the results were in, all three earned their certifications. Joe's smile would have powered the Las Vegas strip for a week. He could've just let the tide drag him out to sea, but instead, he kept swimming.

Authentic values and the stories we tell about them form the foundation of culture.

Peter Drucker coined the famous axiom, "Culture eats strategy for breakfast." Simon Sinek says that culture is a group of people with a common set of values and beliefs.[13]

One might conclude that successfully executing a strategy relies on a group of people with a common set of values. Most leaders understand that a strong and healthy culture is essential to a thriving organization. What doesn't happen as often is the hard work that is needed to clearly define the values that anchor culture and the effort to incorporate those values into the organization.

As I discussed in the previous section, your higher purpose needs to be authentically you. To be worth anything, your values should also come from your heart. If you are taking over a business without a set of values, or you're starting a new organization, those values are likely to be in tune with your own personal values.

If you haven't clearly articulated your own values in writing, then I recommend that you do it now. If culture is a group of people with a common set of values, and culture is the bedrock of an organization, how do you know if you will thrive in an organization if you cannot articulate your own values and those of the group of people you are committing yourself to? How will you clearly explain what is important in your family? How will you honor your own values as you live your life?

I've asked hundreds of interviewees to tell me about their values. I usually say something like, "If you were starting your own business, what words would you put on the wall to tell everyone what the culture was all about?" From entry level to senior leadership positions, I never heard a clear and concise answer to that question. Based on that experience, maybe few people ever even consider the answer. It left me wondering about how they would know if our organization was the right one for them.

Many companies write down their values. Having a set of values fails when those words are not authentic. They are often crafted by committee and vetted by marketing, hung on the wall and posted on the website, and that's where the effort ends. To reach full power, values have to come off the wall and into peoples' hearts and minds. To do that, we must accomplish something that is difficult to do: we have to simplify our values to a few words—or ideally an image or a story—and provide varying levels of detail to back up those words.

> To reach full power, values have to come off the wall and into peoples' hearts and minds.

If you are starting to craft your values, I recommend the "hot pen technique." We came across this process when we attended training on visioning, and it worked well there. "Hot pen" means just sit down and write what comes from your heart. Don't think, don't edit, just write. What is really important to you in life? What makes your blood boil? What gives you comfort and peace? What behaviors do you want your children to learn from you and hold dearly? What are you glad that your parents instilled in you? A blank sheet of paper may be daunting. The thought of coming up with a few words that encapsulate your culture will likely scare you. I recommend that you try to just write from your heart and see what appears.

As with visioning, write "DRAFT" in big letters at the top. Hot pen should only take 15–30 minutes. Set it down, take a breath, get a beverage, and then read what came out of you. Circle the things that jump off the page. Don't get too crazy about wordsmithing yet. Authenticity comes from the heart. We're not marketing yet; we're trying to articulate what's inside of us.

I'm betting that after a few edits, you can start involving more people. A lot of folks go through visioning with a big group, right up front. Some might even outsource this to consultants. Personally, I think it needs to start with the leader. The leader needs to be the guardian of the values and needs to able to genuinely express what they mean. Bringing others in on the exercise is helping to clarify them, ensure they fit the organization, and begin the process of how to communicate them.

> The leader needs to be the guardian of the values and needs to able to genuinely express what they mean.

When I first hung words on the wall, there were too many. I didn't think so at the time. I thought I needed to clearly explain what I meant, so the values first appeared as several sentences on each value. I've seen others do the same thing. Maybe I hang around with too many engineers and not enough marketing people, because I didn't realize that I had to distill the values down to a few words in order to get them in people's heads.

This is when I wish I had read Chip and Dan Heath's book *Made to Stick*. I was making a common mistake. As the Heaths write, "People are tempted to tell you everything, with perfect accuracy, right up front, when they should be giving you just enough info to be useful, then a little more, then a little more. . . . If a message can't be used to make predictions or decisions, it is without value, no matter how accurate or comprehensive it is."[14] We're looking for the memorable headline at this point. Accuracy and completeness come later. We need to make them simple enough so everyone can remember them.

Our attention span is ever shorter. We have access to all

the world's knowledge on our phones. We don't have to remember much, and most of us don't. We remember obscure things but forget the important things. If we want our values to unite the organization, we must find a way to embed triggers that can be remembered. I suggest that you have five words at most. Distill your values to five words or less, and you have a shot at using them to trigger the deeper meaning and creating a framework for culture.

Remember my banking software friend and his purpose that was so surprisingly compelling? He did the same thing with values. He came up with four words, then expressed those four words as the four quadrants of his Roman shield. With one picture, he united purpose and values and made it easy for everyone involved with his business to understand the foundation of his culture. People remember pictures, stories, and songs. Coming up with five words is hard. Coming up with a picture is even harder. The effort is worth it. Do your best to whittle it down to the memorable core.

Next, we need to build on the few words or the picture that triggers our connection to our values. Nobody can really create a rich description of what their culture is with just five words. The words are triggers for the deeper meaning. The words we choose for our business mean what most people would assume when they see the words, but they also mean a lot more. Before we explain the full meaning, though, we need another layer—one that can provide a quick definition of what that value means to flesh out the trigger a bit more.

In their book, the Heaths talk about the Commander's Intent in the Army. No plan survives contact with the enemy.

No sales plan survives contact with the customer. No lesson plan survives contact with teenagers. And no set of values will become actionable with your team unless it is simple. Life is complicated and unpredictable. The best plans often go out the window when unforeseen things happen. A simple statement of intent helps ensure we remember what's important when life happens.

A simple statement of intent helps ensure we remember what's important when life happens.

Commander's Intent should be short and simple. Most of us tend to provide too much information that clutters the point of a simple intent. I love the Heaths' example of how best to explain what a pomelo is:

1. A pomelo is the largest citrus fruit. The rind is very thick but soft and easy to peel away. The resulting fruit has a light yellow to coral pink flesh and can vary from juicy to slightly dry and from seductively spicy-sweet to tangy and tart.

2. A pomelo is basically a supersized grapefruit with a very thick and soft rind.[15]

Hopefully you agree that number two is much better than number one. If not, you may be an engineer. It may be difficult to create such a short and snappy description. Don't sweat it too much. All you want to do at this point is write a short definition of what this word means to you. This will be useful for hanging on the wall, posting online, and putting on job descriptions. Ours eventually were:

1. **Truth.** Open, honest and ethical behavior, seek the truth, face up to challenges, don't hide failure or assign blame.
2. **Service.** Create an amazing end-to-end experience for customers—internal and external. Be a servant leader. Serve the community.
3. **Trust.** Earn freedom and responsibility by being accountable and trustworthy, take ownership, trust your team, walk the talk.
4. **Heart.** Genuinely care, respect others, listen and be open minded, look out for your team, make our world better, play like a pro.
5. **Relentless.** We are tenacious and resilient, we will not fail each other or the customer, we relentlessly improve.

We felt that we had to build more layers of description so we could really dig into the behaviors we wanted. If I imagine myself as the sheriff in a small town in the Old West, it's not enough to say: "Leave your guns at the edge of town and don't bring them into the saloon." I would need to explain why that is important and inspire people to join the effort of building our workplace. We created a one-page explanation of each value and several pages with more detail on how we applied those values in our business to make them authentic. This is like going from the book title to the jacket and then to the chapters. The cover captures your interest, the jacket draws you in, and the story hooks your heart.

There are so many demands on our time that we need options. Maybe all you have time for are the *Cliff's Notes*. Maybe that's the level of depth you are comfortable committing to at the moment. A new recruit isn't likely to read fifteen pages about our values, but we can post one-page summaries that are more digestible.

I think a good bit of management is removing excuses. If we expend the effort required to describe our culture to any reasonably engaged adult, then it's nearly impossible to legitimately complain that the culture stinks.

I eventually adopted the habit of meeting with every new hire shortly after their first day. I had a couple of simple messages to deliver. First, don't do anything you're uncomfortable doing just because someone told you to. Question that and keep questioning until you get to my boss. Second, our culture depends on you. We've done our job by clearly explaining how we want things to be around here. Now it's in your hands. The CEO isn't the culture; the culture is what the people decide it will be. This is another reason why it's important for you to clearly describe what you want; if you don't, you will end up delegating that to someone else, and your only chance of getting the culture you want is if, by some miracle, that person has the same values.

> The CEO isn't the culture; the culture is what the people decide it will be.

The layered approach is difficult and takes time. The words can help put the basics of our values into everyone's heads. The longer descriptions can help the concepts sink in and capture our hearts. Weaving the values into the fabric of the business helps to make them habits.

Values should be visible. Okay, maybe they don't have to

be tattooed on your body in permanent ink. But they should be in your face. Yes, they should be hung up in every conference room and put on your website,

Weaving the values into the fabric of the business helps to make them habits.

but they should also be in big letters on the wall. The triggers should be there in the background all the time, subliminally reminding us about who we are and who we want to be. We put them on our one-page Company Alignment, on our job descriptions, and everywhere else we can work them in.

We need to teach our values. New employee orientation walks our team members through each value, from basic meaning to deeper meaning. We need to start embedding them in memory. If you can't make all of your values fit in one neat picture, can you find a picture for each value? For Truth, we use a still of Jack Nicholson from *A Few Good Men*—yes, you CAN handle the Truth. And for Heart, it's Gordon Gekko from *Wall Street*—greed is most certainly not good. For Relentless, we used a number of images, from Wile E. Coyote to *Dog the Bounty Hunter*, but the best picture told the story of a team member running his first 10k. You can see and feel Relentless from the look on his face.

Pictures put the word triggers in our heads, and stories cement the concept in our hearts. Like the story from the opening of this section, stories connect us to values in a special way. Joe's story wasn't just about being Relentless, it was also about Heart, Service, Trust, and Truth.

I think most companies try to incorporate their values into hiring. If culture is a group of people with a common set of values, then we should be discussing whether there is a match before we bring that new individual into our group. Patrick Lencioni says in his book *The Ideal Team Player*, "The most unhappy people in a company are the ones who don't fit the culture and are allowed to stay. They know they don't belong. Deep down inside they don't want to be there."[16]

> Pictures put the word triggers in our heads and stories cement the concept in our hearts.

Like the characters in Lencioni's book, we started to think about the virtues of people that fit our culture. The five words and their meanings helped, but we also needed to think about adjectives that describe our best cultural fit.

Humility is not one of our five values, but over time we realized it was a critical trait for a good fit. Servant leaders and people dedicated to service require humility. Once we can describe what we're looking for, we can design interview questions to ferret that out, then we can train individuals to interview specifically for cultural fit.

The Ideal Team Player also cast new light on why we found humility so important. Lencioni describes how being humble is critical to teamwork. It takes humility to genuinely get onto the same side of the table. He writes, "Great team players lack excessive ego or concerns about status."[17]

The most impactful thing for me personally was Lencioni's view that people who lack self-confidence do not demonstrate humility. I've always thought of myself as humble and never connected self-esteem to "unhealthy humility." He goes on to write, "People who lack self-confidence . . . tend to discount their own talents and contributions. . . . While they are certainly not arrogant, their lack of understanding of their own worth is also a violation of humility. Truly humble people do not see themselves as greater than they are, but neither do they discount their talents and contributions."[18]

It takes humility to genuinely get onto the same side of the table.

This is especially important in leaders, because they may not advocate for their own ideas or call attention to problems. Now we have to think about healthy humility in our interviewing, and we may have unwittingly hurt our culture by seeking out humble people without testing for self-esteem at the same time.

Interviewing for virtues, values, and cultural fit is not groundbreaking—there are many companies that do this much better than we do. But there are also a lot of companies that don't even think about figuring out cultural fit or interviewing for it. Remove the excuses for having a negative culture.

Finally, leaders have to demonstrate our values, and we have to connect difficult decisions to our values. Leaders need to recognize when people demonstrate our values in action and call them out or point out when they don't. In those occasional instances when there's a fork in the road, we need to stop and consider whether our values direct us down one lane or the other. The easy decision is to tell yourself what you want to hear. Values tell us what we need to hear.

I recently came across a company called Atomic Object. I don't know much about the company, though I do love how they present their values. And at this time, they are the only company I've seen with the value Give a Shit. Give a Shit is easy to remember (maybe even unforgettable) and it's clearly authentic. I also love how each value is explained through the words of colleagues and other stakeholders. The layers are there, from a few words to stories that draw in the head and the heart. The positivity of these values shines through, and I'm guessing that they have woven these values into many organizational practices as the foundation of a good culture.

> The easy decision is to tell yourself what you want to hear. Values tell us what we need to hear.

A clear and authentic set of values has power. It's difficult to measure the return on this investment. We can use employee retention as a proxy, but it isn't a pure cause-result measure. I can't tell my younger self that I invested X and got Y out of the investment in a strong set of values. I can confidently say that it is something that made my life easier as a leader: knowing that we made the effort to help everyone understand what kind of business we were trying to build and engage them in the job of protecting and building our culture. It helped us recruit the right people. It created a fulfilling workplace. It built trust and relationships. And it established a clear fence line that made it easier to provide our colleagues with autonomy.

Bringing It Home

What can a clear set of values do for your organization at home? Another question I like to ask an interviewee is what they took with them when they left their parents' home. What values did their parents instill in them? I ask this because I find those things are hard-wired into most people. To this day, I recognize the positive and negative traits that my parents instilled in me—whether they meant to or not. I meet a lot of people who can describe how they learned a strong work ethic from their parents—the memories are so fresh it's like they left home yesterday. My parents clearly demonstrated faith in God, and I took that with me—maybe not exactly the way they practiced, but it was *my* faith. What words hang on your wall to trigger the behaviors you want to see and develop? Does your home team know what these values are and why you hold them dearly? Are you equipping them with a set of positive tools that will help them live joyfully, or filling their bags up with things that will hamper them their whole lives?

I thought about my transition away from being a CEO for a long time, and I had a hard time figuring out where to head next. Then I came across the book *Designing Your Life* by Bill Burnett and Dave Evans. The subtitle of this book is "How to Build a Well-Lived, Joyful Life." Sign me up. One of the initial exercises they recommend is to describe your views about life and work. What you deeply believe about work and life are the foundation of your values. They write, "You can't chart a course of one straight line—you tack according to what the winds and conditions allow.... I won't always know where I'm going—but I can always know whether I'm going in the right direction."[19]

> A well-lived and joyful life is possible when we have values that act as our compass.

A well-lived and joyful life is possible when we have values that act as our compass. I think that a compass is one of the best gifts we can give ourselves, and I'm certain that creating a moral compass for an organization is essential to success.

TAKEAWAYS

- Authentic values and the stories we tell about them form the foundation of culture. Culture is a group of people with a common set of values and beliefs.
- A great strategy is not worth much if it cannot be realized. "Culture eats strategy for breakfast" means that you can't succeed without a unified group of people, even with a great plan.
- A clear set of values unites people. It forms the basis of trust and confidence. It is intensely difficult to operate within an organization whose values do not align with your own.
- Like purpose, values need to be authentic. Values need to be distilled down to a few words that are easy for everyone to remember and rally around.
- The hard work is creating layers of detail under the simple triggers and aligning everything in your organization around these shared values to create a solid foundation based on trust.

QUESTIONS AND ACTIONS

- If you were starting your own business, what words would you hang on the wall to help establish a clear and consistent culture?

- Think about a time when you were part of an organization whose values were very different from your own. What impact did that have on your performance, trust, comfort, and health?

- Have you captured your own values in writing? If not, how do you go about determining if the organization you work within shares your own set of values?

- Does your family have a clear set of values that is understood by everyone? How are your own values different than your parents' values?

- Do you believe your current organization's values are authentic? What could you do within your own team to authentically align with the organization's values?

CHAPTER 3

AUTHENTIC LEADERSHIP

All leaders should serve at the
pleasure of those they lead.

Older me
@grayhairandscars

I told #mom what you did last night.

3:42 PM Sep 23, 1985

[heart] 0 [comment] 1,027 people are Tweeting about this.

---

uthenticity is probably not the first word you think of associating with leadership. Trust, respect, caring, selflessness . . . those *should be* some of the first words we associate with leadership. Transparency from leadership is the building block of trust and all the good that flows from there.

> Transparency from leadership is the building block of trust and all the good that flows from there.

One of the ways I tried to be transparent was to make my calendar public. It helped other people schedule time with me and put credibility around our Open Door Policy. It was a way of saying that I have nothing to hide and encouraged people to be similarly transparent about how they spend their workday. It added credibility to our claim that we'd openly share anything about the business with any colleague unless we were bound by confidentiality.

And maybe it led to one of my most difficult days as a leader. One day, a colleague I had hardly met tapped on the door and asked if I had a minute. "Sure, come on in," I said. She replied, "Well, I'm resigning, today's my last day, and I just wanted to let you know that my boss has been harassing me because I know about the affair he's having with someone on our team. Oh, and let me introduce you to my husband, who's here to pick me up. He's the VP of HR at a company just down the street from here." "Hmm," I said, "Can I take back my first answer?"

No, I didn't really say that. I listened, shocked, as she told me the story. As shaken as I was, I answered her questions honestly. I spoke about the culture we sought to create. I promised to investigate the situation. Harassment of any kind is not tolerated. If confirmed, her supervisor's behavior would be dealt with immediately. And I meant every word. Our culture is very important to me, and nothing is more important than integrity and creating a safe environment for our people to thrive. The idea that one of our leaders could do the things she told me about was disgusting.

She looked at her husband, who hadn't said a word.

They looked at me, thanked me for my time, and asked me to let them know what my investigation uncovered. At that moment, I was convinced that I would be hearing from her attorney very soon.

We did what we said we were going to do and immediately conducted an investigation. The supervisor initially denied everything. Then denied it again, and again. Then he realized he was caught and the evidence against him was clear. He apologized for his behavior and asked for another chance. He was critical to our operation. He led a team that was responsible for delivering all of the revenue for that division, and he was the face of that team to our customers. Losing him was going to create financial issues for our business. It was one of the easiest decisions I ever made. He was let go immediately. Trust, Truth, Service, Heart . . . those are just not words on the wall, they are the values we live by. No amount of profit is worth our soul. What he did violated everything we believe in.

No amount of profit is worth our soul.

We cleaned up the mess. Then I called my ex-colleague back and told her and her husband about the investigation and what we did. I didn't call my attorney first, and I hadn't heard anything yet from her attorney. Regardless of what she was going to do next, I felt they needed to hear that we meant what we said, we sincerely regretted what happened to her, and we would continue to do everything we could to prevent it from happening again. I told her how much I appreciated her having the courage and responsibility to come to me and explain what was happening on my watch.

She told me that she thought our culture was genuine, and that, with the exception of her supervisor, our leadership and our people seemed to walk the walk. She and her husband had talked about suing our company, and they wanted to see how we would handle the situation before doing that. Would we be true to ourselves, or would we sacrifice our values for profit? They could smell whitewash a mile away, and they were convinced that we were being true. That was the last time I heard from her.

None of that happened because my calendar was public. It was because we were genuine and transparent. The meetings we had to investigate the situation and clean up after it were not public. There were plenty of things on my calendar that couldn't be made public without creating undue distraction or violating confidentiality. Everyone has private appointments on their calendar. There's a big difference between looking at someone's calendar and seeing a few private appointments or another's calendar where it says nothing but "I'm busy."

When I became the enemy (read *management*), I still thought of myself as the same person. Becoming the president of a small company came as a surprise, and I didn't have time to think about what that meant. I was completely focused on trying to build a successful business. It took me many years to realize that people perceived me differently, just because I had a title.

So, another thing I would tell my younger self is to be more aware of how colleagues view you when you have the title of manager, leader, president, or owner. The title immediately erects walls and creates distance. When you walk in as the CEO, people start taking stuff out of that suitcase of past perceptions and sticking labels on you. A little transparency goes a long way toward helping keep some of those labels from sticking.

Traditional awareness of leadership is usually about power and ego. "I'm in charge here, so you'd better do what I tell you to do." It's about trappings, perks, and special treatment. Unfortunately, I think many people aspire to be leaders so they can tell people what to do and be respected. As an "employee," I often didn't feel a lot of respect; I felt like a cog in the machine. None of us should have to be the CEO to be respected, and none of us should feel threatened by the authority conveyed to the leader of the organization.

The foundation of our leadership training became Servant Leadership, because great leadership starts there. It helps shrink from both sides the distance between manager and employee. Robert Greenleaf coined the phrase in a collection of essays he wrote on the subject between 1967 and 1987. His ten critical characteristics should be required reading for any leader.

Greenleaf said the test of servant leadership is: "Do those served grow as persons? Do they, *while being served*, become healthier, wiser, freer, more autonomous, more likely themselves to become servants? *And*, what is the effect on the least privileged in society; will they benefit, or, at least, not be further deprived?"[20] True leadership emerges from those whose primary motivation is a deep desire to help others.

Servant leadership turns management from power and perks into responsibility and care. There are many things we can do as leaders to promote transparency, universal respect, and open dialogue. It may be tempting to stand on the pedestal of your title and wrap yourself in power and perks. Like many temptations, though, that is a road to nowhere.

Servant leadership turns management from power and perks into responsibility and care.

Servant leadership tells us that we serve at the pleasure of those we lead. Haven't we all seen movies and television shows where characters serve at the pleasure of the president? Imagine if all leaders treated their titles as responsibility to others rather than the power to do what they want. Would I have felt better in the corporations I worked at if the CEO felt he reported to employees, customers, suppliers, and communities as much as he reported to the board and shareholders?

James Robbins says it well in *Nine Minutes on Monday*: "Because leadership hinges on your ability to influence people, you want to do everything you can to build trust . . . you may be able to hire employees' hands, but you will never employ their hearts without trust, and without heart, performance will always fall short of potential . . . only 11 percent of employees strongly agree that their managers show consistency between words and actions."[21] He advised leaders not to underestimate how closely people watch your example. When managers lead with integrity and consistency of example, it creates a solid foundation that employees can rely on. The key ingredient is time—trust is built up layer by layer.

I've used a jumble of words to describe good leadership in this section: transparent, selfless, truthful, balanced, moral.

Let's roll all of those up in a ball and call it authenticity. You can go a long way back in time to *Hamlet* to see where this starts: "To thine own self be true," and all that. While the concept itself isn't new, research about its impact in the workplace has blossomed in the last twenty years. Maybe it's the corporate scandals, the housing crash, the repeated lapses in ethical judgment. As the authors of a very good paper on the subject said, "Organizational stakeholders appear to be much less tolerant of inconsistencies between leaders' espoused principles, values, and conduct and are expecting those leaders to operate at higher levels of integrity."[22]

This paper cites quite a bit of growing evidence that authentic leadership achieves positive and enduring organizational outcomes. In other words, authentic leadership is essential for a thriving organization. It leads to higher levels of individual performance, engagement, self-esteem, well-being, and friendliness. It leads to greater levels of motivation and autonomy. It encourages corporate social responsibility. Authenticity is what followers want to see from leaders.

At any level, people wonder how the leader is spending her day. We've become so conditioned to leadership being behind closed doors. One of my favorite songs in the musical *Hamilton* expresses the frustration of not being in "The Room Where It Happens." Power is opaque decision making. Leaders don't have to explain themselves. . . .until everything goes wrong, and then there's a whole lot of explaining.

Why not share what you can about the process and involve the team more? Just the other day, I was talking to another CEO and I asked about the culture he wanted to create. He started with transparency. Every Friday he sends a short note to his team letting them know good news, bad news, and key decisions, and it finishes with gratitude. His leadership team is in the loop on key decisions as a group and doesn't spend their time arguing about who was in the room where it happened. People become more aligned, because the message is consistent. People become more understanding of mistakes and failures, because they were in the loop on the decision when it was made and not spending time second-guessing.

There are many simple things we can do to be authentic about our responsibilities to our stakeholders and to treat our colleagues as we would any other important stakeholder. Later on, you'll hear about an Accelerator Practice called Culture Council, which is essentially an employee advisory board. Treating the Culture Council with the same respect as the board of directors sends the right message. There are opportunities every day to demonstrate that you respect all of your stakeholders and that you are approachable and genuine. Humility is critical to servant leadership and good teamwork. The minute we start thinking about how we can distance ourselves by climbing on the pedestal of power is the beginning of our fall from grace.

> The minute we start thinking about how we can distance ourselves by climbing on the pedestal of power is the beginning of our fall from grace.

The User Manual is another accelerator that can help leaders build bridges and reduce the distance created when we accept leadership. Open-Book Finance has many benefits, one of which is sharing financial information that is often kept private. The Position Alignment is a great way to be transparent about your roles and responsibilities. Creating and publishing my Reflection felt like the ultimate opening of the kimono. You'll hear about all of these if you keep reading. I'm sure there are many more ways I haven't heard about yet that demonstrate authenticity, encourage approachability, and build trust. I would tell my younger self that being approachable and authentic helped me avoid more than one left hook to the temple.

One thing we still need to do a better job of is to teach our leaders to ask better questions. Looking back, I definitely did too much telling and not enough asking.

The art of asking becomes more difficult as status increases. Our culture emphasizes that leaders must be wiser, set direction, and articulate values, all of which predisposes them to tell rather than ask. Yet it is leaders who will need Humble Inquiry most, because complex, interdependent tasks will require building positive, trusting relationships with subordinates to facilitate good upward communication. And without that, organizations can be neither effective nor safe.[23]

Teaching and practicing humble inquiry should be added to our list of positive practices to break down walls.

If I believe and act like I serve at the pleasure of all stakeholders, then I hold myself to a higher standard of performance, regardless of whether I am in a high-profile public company or working for a small private one. In so doing, I demonstrate humility and openness. I create transparency and respect for the team, which build relationships. And hopefully that example is taken up across the organization at all levels.

People today have a greater hunger for authenticity. I was recently talking with a friend who went to work for a big corporation after graduating from engineering school. Then COVID-19 hit. What bothered him most about how his employer responded was the lack of transparency. When times are tough, that's when people *really* need honesty. They need to be in the room where it happens, because there's a lot more riding on the decisions being made. Did the senior leadership take a pay cut before laying off employees? Does leadership have a plan for what actions we think we're going to take at different stages of this crisis? His leaders called a meeting to take questions, but never ended up answering any of them. As anyone who watched the debates leading into the 2020 election knows, NOT answering any questions is worse than not calling the meeting in the first place.

> When times are tough, that's when people *really* need honesty.

I'm proud of our team for how they handled the outbreak in March 2020. The first thing leadership decided was that letting people go during a crisis like COVID-19 was the last resort—better for everyone to take pay cuts than to have to put good people out of work at a time like that. Beyond the humanity of that decision was the practical and financial: at some point things would return to normal and it was very hard to find that talent in the first place. They ran the numbers and told the team what would happen if sales fell to different levels. The first level would trigger pay cuts for senior leaders, a hiring freeze, and discretionary spending cuts. No layoffs. The second level would increase the cuts for the highest paid, initiate cuts for the next level, and increase the belt tightening. And so on. We were able to communicate that we wouldn't have to put anyone out of work unless things were worse than our most dire projections. We upped our transparency and kept it high during the crisis, and we felt like that was an oasis in the desert for our people.

Bringing It Home

How can parents demonstrate authenticity as leaders of the family? We clearly seek transparency from our kids, and it seems that we seek it much more today than when I was running around until dark without a cell phone or any other sort of tracking device. The transparency desired by parents changes with age because maybe we don't really want to know what they

Transparency creates approachability.

are doing in their teens or at college. And maybe after they're married we just want to know when the grandkids are coming to visit. But does authenticity with your kids build stronger relationships and keep you out of trouble at home like it does at work? Do your kids want more transparency from you about what's going on at home?

With my parents, I can't say that they felt very approachable. I had bosses that I felt more comfortable going to than my dad. I would only go to Dad if there was just no other way around it. As a parent and a manager, I don't think it would go well if I'm creating the same feeling. Transparency creates approachability. This is different than being your child's friend. My job as parent and a manager is not to be their best friend; it's to be their guardian, coach, and mentor. And I don't think I can do that very well if I'm not approachable. While my dad was not very approachable, he was authentic—he walked his talk, even if he didn't talk very much.

It feels like we've lived a different story with my kids, though I'm sure that's due to the efforts of my wonderful wife more than me. We only had two kids, and they were mature and wonderful from day one. We grew up in different times and in a much better situation than my dad. We involved our kids at whatever level they seemed to be comfortable with. They asked questions, and we answered them honestly. If we didn't feel it was appropriate to answer at that time, we said so. If all of my relationships at work went as well as our relationship with our kids, then I'd have a lot less gray hair now. The same goes if maybe if I consistently treated my colleagues at work like I treated my daughters, instead of being "the boss." I can't advise anyone to apply transparency and approachability at home, except for Younger Me, and I'd encourage him not to change a thing about how we did it.

I'd like to finish this chapter on authentic leadership with a quote from the book *True to Yourself* by Mark Albion:

> As a business leader, your job is not a popularity contest. It's to do the right thing and help people

become the best they can be. . . . You must let go of control to have honesty and transparency inside and outside the company. It's the only way to treat people like grown-ups so you can develop trust and build leadership in the company.[24]

TAKEAWAYS

- Authentic leadership leads to higher levels of performance, engagement, self-esteem, well-being, motivation, autonomy, and respect.
- Transparency from leadership is the building block of trust and all the good that flows from there. People are drawn to authentic and transparent leadership because it creates a solid foundation for lasting and successful relationships.
- Treating employees and children with respect and involving them in decisions can help them become more confident and independent.
- Traditional leadership driven by power and ego creates a chasm between leadership and team. Genuinely approaching leadership from a mindset of service shrinks the gap, connects leadership to critical information, and conveys a respect to the team that increases engagement.
- Leaders that serve at the pleasure of all stakeholders hold themselves to a higher standard of performance. They demonstrate humility and openness,

transparency and respect for the team, and set an example that is taken up across the organization at all levels.

QUESTIONS AND ACTIONS

- What's preventing you from being more transparent with your team?

- What could you do to shrink the gap between you and your team that is naturally created by title and position?

- Are you listening enough? Learn more about humble inquiry so you can practice it. Keep a journal of what you learned by listening that you might not have picked up without listening more.

- As a parent, are you demonstrating servant leadership? Are you (appropriately) bringing your children into the room where it happens?

- Think about a time when you weren't authentic—when you tried to avoid an issue, cover it up, or put a spin on it. How did that impact the people around you? What did it do to you?

CHAPTER 4

LEADERSHIP TRAINING

You're only as good as your leaders, and they
need to know what good looks like.

I went back to school to get my MBA because I wanted a way
to escape a purely technical career. I never imagined I would
lead a business. I certainly did not understand that I needed
a lot more training about motivating and leading people. As a
result, despite the MBA, there were many aspects of running
a business where I felt completely at sea. And nothing stood
out to me more than a lack of understanding about what good
leadership looked like.

So, if I was at sea about that, what about the rest of our
leaders? Only a few of them had business degrees, and they
didn't study leadership either. Because we are a technology
business, almost nobody had a psychology degree. Most of
our people were engineers and programmers—emotional
intelligence was not in abundance.

Think back on your own career for a moment. How many great leaders did you work for? How many of us had great models for our own leadership? Where do we learn about good leadership?

As we grew beyond ten or twenty employees, I started to learn some very hard lessons. I recognized that I needed to learn some new skills and I needed to learn them quickly. I started reading anything I could get my hands on about leadership and business—many were not helpful.

The first leadership book I read was actually a great parenting book: *How to Talk So Kids Will Listen and Listen So Kids Will Talk* by Adele Faber and Elaine Mazlish. I was even more driven to learn about parenting than I was about leading a group of adults. My daughters were very young at the time, and as I read that book, I saw and felt the workplace more than home. Many of the issues addressed in the book looked a lot like what I was experiencing at the office. And when I tried Adele's advice, it actually worked at the office on the adult "children" in my care.

I have always learned better by writing things down. As I read books about parenting and leadership, I wrote summaries of them for myself. Over time, I made those summaries available to our leadership team and friends. I wrote a summary of Faber and Mazlish's book in 2000. Twenty years later, what I wrote then is still very much on my mind:

> We have built something special here in part because we try not to treat employees as such in the traditional sense—we try not to police them, control

them, yell at them, punish them, or otherwise treat employees like most corporations do. Instead, our culture focuses on treating employees as owners, respecting their abilities and thoughts, talking openly with them, helping them discover who they are professionally and how they fit in the company team. We try hard to break down the walls between departments and between "employee" and "management," because working together makes life a lot more pleasant for everyone. This book recommends the same type of practices and techniques between parents and children. It is based upon the premise that parents shouldn't treat kids "like children" all the time, but instead, treat them as human beings struggling to cope with their own set of issues. As parents and managers, it is our responsibility to help them, set firm boundaries for their protection, set clear expectations and goals, talk with them, and respect their needs, often putting their needs in front of our own.

Good parenting and good leadership have a lot in common. Some twenty years later, I enhanced that lesson after reading how Simon Sinek discussed this link in *Leaders Eat Last.* "Every single employee is someone's son or someone's daughter. Like a parent, a leader of a company is responsible for their precious lives...Letting someone into an

> Good parenting and good leadership have a lot in common.

organization is like adopting a child." Just as a parent can't buy the love of their children with gifts, a company can't buy loyalty or engagement with money."[25]

First and foremost is genuinely caring about the person in your care. Good parents don't look at their children as human resources to be exploited for their own benefit. Good parents put their children first—not by spoiling them, but by ensuring they are nurtured and cared for. Good parents and good leaders, challenge their charges to be the best they can be. We don't teach this explicitly at work. But I love win-wins, and if we can equip leaders with best practices that help at work and at home, then I'm even more willing to make the investment.

Faber and Mazlish's book explains that there is a direct connection between how kids feel and how they behave. "When kids feel right, they'll behave right." By accepting their feelings, children will feel right. However, parents usually deny kids' feelings. This confuses and frustrates them and causes them not to trust their own feelings or respect others.[26]

This is empathy and active listening. How much of those two things have you experienced at work? More and more though, we see courses being offered on exactly those positive practices at work.

In 2000 I started to send our leadership team articles and book summaries. This seemed to be a "build it and they will come" approach. I realized that we needed to bring the horses to the trough if we wanted them to drink. We took the most impactful books and packaged them up into basic leadership training. We asked all of our leaders to take the training and encouraged them to read the foundational books (or at the very least, the *Cliff's Notes*).

The next natural step for us was to offer this training to any colleague who wanted it. We encouraged everyone to attend these voluntary lunch-and-learns for two very good reasons. First, we never know where our next great leader will come from. We could often iden-tify high potential individuals by their attendance and contribu-tions at these short sessions. Sec-ond, we encouraged all colleagues to attend the training so they could understand how we wanted our leaders to behave. We wanted them to help us hold our own leaders accountable.

> I believe that leaders are made, and not born, so good leaders need training and feedback.

I believe that leaders are made, and not born, so good leaders need training and feedback. We all know that teaching and learning is very different than practicing and mastery. If we could get our colleagues to give managers targeted and re-spectful feedback about their leadership, we are on the same side of the table, working together as a unit to create better versions of both manager and employee. Of course, the re-lationship has to be in place and the overall climate has to support the ability of that little plant to grow and thrive. If it does, the fruit is nutritious.

I was lucky enough to become involved in two great leadership development groups: Young Entrepreneurs Orga-nization (YEO) and Young Presidents Organization (YPO). One of the cornerstones of both organizations is the concept of Forum: a subset of about ten leaders who regularly meet in complete confidentiality. This is basically an emotional support group for business leaders. It is also focused on continuous learning opportunities.

As we committed ourselves to training leaders, we adopted a version of Forum. As a group, we met regularly to learn together. Annually, this involved a two-day, in-person session with all of our leaders. We combined business discussions with training. Together, we learned the power of creating a vision and how to manage change, among many other things. It was my hope that our leaders would begin to form bonds with their peers like we did in Forum. In doing so, leaders could seek help from peers on issues that they may have felt uncomfortable discussing with their own manager.

Of course, the dynamic between peers in business is very different. YPO is very careful about competitors and suppliers being part of the same Forum group. Leaders in business are almost always suppliers or competitors in some sense. I'd like to believe we could put that internal competition aside, but we need to be realistic: Forum at work would not have the same dynamic. All the same, the learning is critical, and if we helped build better relationships between leaders, then it's a win.

Learning is a funny thing. If you ask most people whether they want to learn and develop, they will usually answer with a resounding yes. If you ask most companies, they want a culture of learning that creates better versions of people (their most important asset). In reality, though, we may say we want to learn, but we routinely short-circuit the learning cycle: Plan, Act, Reflect, Discover, as shown in Figure 4.1.[27] This cycle drives learning and mastery. What I've witnessed, though, is that we spend about 25 percent of our time planning and

75 percent of our time acting. Work is a treadmill of Plan-Act with little time for Reflection and Discovery. In many workplaces, taking time for those activities is seen as goofing off. In many places, asking people to take some time to reflect results in quite a bit of eye rolling. "Are you kidding me? You think I have time for that? Have you seen how busy I am?"

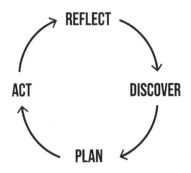

Figure 4.1: Plan, Act, Reflect, Discover

The Forum concept gave us the ability to teach good leadership to our team. This was the Plan part—providing foundational books, summaries, and tools. Forum also gave us opportunities to regularly reflect and discover. We would bring up issues that we were facing and discuss how to practice good leadership in resolving the issue. We brought these leadership principles into our policy making. We encouraged feedback in the 1-2-1 Check-ins. We transformed our performance appraisal into mandated time for reflection. We're not patting ourselves on the back, and I'm not saying we figured all of this out. We are a long, long way from perfect. A lot of the battle is the journey and creating the space and environment to allow these practices to take hold.

The way we described the foundation of good leadership is:

- **Servant leadership** (*The Power of Servant Leadership* by Robert K. Greenleaf): Put people's needs ahead of your own. Leadership is a responsibility to care for others, not a perk. Set clear goals, and a firm fence line, then trust the team to figure it out. Help people become their best selves.

- **Focus on strengths** (*First, Break All the Rules* by Marcus Buckingham and Curt Coffman): Look for the good in people and develop it. Help identify peoples' footpaths and superhighways. Be consistent, yet treat everyone as an individual. Define the right outcomes and stick to them. Look beyond job title.

- **Motivate and care** (*Nine Minutes on Monday* by James Robbins, *Drive* by Daniel Pink): Autonomy, purpose, and mastery drive people more than money. Genuinely care about people, and they will care, too. Recognize, connect, bring joy and love to work, model good behavior, and grow personally and professionally.

- **Drive engagement** (*Ownership Thinking* by Brad Hams): Good goal setting and metrics drive performance, learning, satisfaction, and well-being and avoid me-centricity, entitlement, and victims. Bring people behind the curtain to engage them in the great game of business.

- **Lead positively** (*True to Yourself* by Mark Albion, *Lift* by Ryan and Robert Quinn): Building a great business is destiny, not destination. Lead with doubt and purpose. Nourish the soil, reflect, have patience, and avoid obsession with size, speed, and publicity. Demonstrate compassion, competence, and commitment.

If you've read chapter 2, you should see something in common here. We're trying to distill our leadership fundamentals down to just a few words to use as triggers. Servant leaders, develop strengths, motivate and care, drive engagement, and inspire. These are our foundational leadership values. There are a few more words in each bullet to help summarize what that means. Each one has at least one book we found to be extremely helpful in defining leadership so you can dive deep (or you can read the *Cliff's Notes*). Then we weave these into our values; one leads to another, that one ties to this one. Then we try to build practices around these concepts so everyone is involved. This isn't just a book, or an experience, or the flavor of the day. It's backed by research, data, and real work situations. It's not complete or perfect, but it is a good foundation to build on. This takes time and consistent effort.

Is it worth the effort? Think back on your own experience with leadership. Think about leaders who frustrated you and made you doubt your abilities or filled your bags with experiences that made coming to work a challenge. Now think about the leader who inspired you and made you a better person. If just one of our leaders can positively impact the life of one of our people, it's worth it.

But if you are a leader yourself, especially if you lead an entire organization, think for a moment about your own leadership team. If you have more than 25 or 50 people under your responsibility, it becomes very difficult to be everyone's leader. You have to delegate that responsibility to others. You know you are only as good as they are. You have likely swept up messes from leaders that don't lead well. You've been surprised by losing good people or poor execution or poor planning. As your team gets bigger, it's harder for you to influence anyone beyond your leadership team. Are you comfortable leaving them on their own to figure out what good leadership looks like?

Good leadership is something you can practice at every level. Nobody in HR is likely to stop you from practicing leadership as we define it. You don't have to adopt everything we did. You can try bits and pieces and see how it fits on you. Or you can discard all of our foundational principles for your own. The key point is that you need to discover what good leadership means to you and be able to explain that to others.

We're still on the journey and studying what good leadership looks like. The books *Nine Minutes on Monday* and *Lift* were not part of the first five; we added them, since they seemed to add depth to what we originally had. Mackey and Sisodia's *Conscious Capitalism* is a fantastic overview of how you create a thriving organization, and I wish I had read it when it was published instead of while I was writing this book. The story of Whole Foods makes it easier to show leadership what thriving looks like and its impact on all stakeholders. There are so many great books out there and many great leaders that have yet to share their secrets. Our reading list can be found in appendix 7.

Bringing It Home

I submit that these leadership practices are just as valuable at home as they would be at the office. In your little town, what does good leadership look like? Do you consider yourself as a Servant Leader, or are your kids there to do your bidding and do what you tell them to do? Do you help them find purpose and meaning, or is their job to get out of the house as soon as possible? Do you look for ways to use autonomy, purpose, and mastery as natural motivators instead of money or punishment? Are they involved in decision-making at an appropriate level? Are they in the room where it happens, whenever possible?

Once you've answered those questions as a parent, think about them again in any other leadership experience you're involved with. Is that how things run on that non-profit board or church council? Does the Little League team operate with that set of values? Leadership opportunities are everywhere you look, yet good leadership is hard to find. Why don't we make it less of a unicorn?

A final word to Younger Me on this topic: I waited too long to adopt this practice. As a result, for years I became frustrated with the failures of our leadership when I should have blamed myself for not teaching people what good leadership looks like. As your organization grows, you will quickly lose the ability to influence it on your own, and you will delegate responsibility for caring about most of your colleagues. No matter how good you are, you will only be as good as your leaders. You owe it to yourself, your leaders, and all of the people in your care to take the time and teach them what good leadership means to you.

TAKEAWAYS

- Few leaders have any formal leadership training. Many people are put into leadership positions based on performance or seniority. Even if they've had leadership training, it's rare to find an organization that has a consistent and published set of leadership beliefs.
- One of my first leadership lessons is that good parenting and good leadership have a lot in common. As parents and leaders, it is our responsibility to help the people in our care, set firm boundaries for their protection, set clear expectations and goals, coach them, and respect them, putting their needs ahead of our own.
- Good leadership needs to be taught and practiced—both are often overlooked. Most people leave their manager, not the company. As an organization grows, it depends more and more on its leaders—the founder/CEO can no longer have contact with everyone. For these reasons and more, an organization's beliefs about good leadership need to be clear and consistent, in much the same way as its values and purpose.
- Good leadership is something that can be practiced at every level. Like any other endeavor, you will make

mistakes—own them and learn from them. Bring good leadership home with you and demonstrate what it looks like to your family.

QUESTIONS AND ACTIONS

- What formal leadership training have you had? What have your leaders had? Do you and your leaders share the same leadership beliefs?

- Think about the best leader you ever had. What made her so wonderful? What were her beliefs about good leadership? Which of those beliefs do you practice as a leader?

- What positive and negative leadership lessons did you learn from your parents? How did those travel with you throughout your career? What lessons are you teaching your children?

- Do you study and practice good leadership as you would any other endeavor you are passionate about? If not, can you truly be delivering on your promise to those you lead?

CHAPTER 5

VISIONING AND CHANGE

If you don't know where you're going, it doesn't
matter which fork in the road you choose.

I held the position of CEO for too long. In retrospect, I'm
not sure anyone should be in charge of anything for more
than twenty years. For one thing, it's hard to look at the
business with a truly fresh perspective after that long. Mainly,
though, I think it's just too exhausting, if you genuinely care.
For me, it might have been easier if I would have adopted a
lot more positive business practices earlier to inject more joy
and to avoid more problems. This is especially true because
I'm an engineer at heart, naturally drawn to the negative point
of view and always in search of a problem. I didn't pick up
techniques for recovery, resilience, and renewal until way too
late in my career.

Visioning is one such positive and hopeful practice that I
would have liked to have adopted sooner, both personally and

professionally. Professionally, for our first years in operation, our vision could be summed up in a word: *survive*. Like a lot of start-ups, it was a long and grinding road to success. Professional visioning might not have come in as handy during that phase, but personal visioning would have been an important tool for staying positive.

Once we achieved stability in our business, we had more choices. It was a joy to realize that we now had to spend time thinking about what we wanted to be in the future other than still being in business. As we really began thinking about creating a vision for our business, we realized we needed to get some training. A CEO who doesn't know about visioning is like a car with square wheels—missing that feature is going to make for a bumpy ride.

Through our connections to the Center for Positive Organizations at the University of Michigan, we heard about ZingTrain, the training business within the Zingerman's family of businesses. In 1982, Zingerman's was a college town delicatessen; years later it became the subject of an article in the magazine *Inc.* called "The Coolest Small Company in America."[28] That article was the inspiration for the author, Bo Burlingham, to write a book about thriving organizations called *Small Giants*.

> A CEO that doesn't know about visioning is like a car with square wheels—missing that feature is going to make for a bumpy ride.

Much of what we learned about visioning and why it's important we learned from Zingerman's. Ari Weinzweig sums up the win-win opportunity from visioning: The more everyone in our group is growing and learning, the better the business is going to be. The more we teach everyone to go after their dreams, the more fulfilling their lives will be. The more fulfilled they feel, the better the quality of their work, and the better the organization will operate.[29]

Nothing engages me more as a leader than a win-win. The most difficult decisions we face are when one of our stakeholders has to sacrifice for another. Lower wages and longer hours may benefit shareholders but hurt colleagues. Bad profits may benefit shareholders and (financially) colleagues but hurt customers. And on and on. But give me a way where everyone wins, at home and at work, and I'm all in. Visioning helps all stakeholders. Individuals can take the practice home to their families. Teams can create a vision for a better workplace. Organizations create a future that is better than the past and engage everyone in making it happen.

Stories and images are the best way to engage people in change. The simple story about the importance of visioning is the scene in *Alice in Wonderland* when Alice encounters the Cheshire Cat at a fork in the road. When she wonders which way she should go, the Cheshire Cat materializes and asks where Alice wants to end up. When Alice says she doesn't know, the Cat replies, "Well, then I guess it doesn't matter which fork you take." Visioning establishes a destination. Without a destination, you are just wandering around, a victim of whatever comes your way. For most people, that simple logic is powerful. If you want some control over where you end up, you need to know where you want to be.

One of the three intrinsic motivators from *Drive* by

Daniel Pink is autonomy. It's having some control over our destiny. We don't want to be cogs in a machine. We want to have the opportunity to control whether we reach our dreams or not. He writes, "Motivation 2.0 assumed that if people had freedom they would shirk [responsibility]. . . . Motivation 3.0 . . . presumes that people *want* to be accountable"—providing control over task, time, technique, and team is the most effective pathway to that destination.[30]

If you want some control over where you end up, you need to know where you want to be.

Yet, oddly enough, many people don't have a specific destination in mind and no real plan for arriving there. It's an odd contradiction that I've witnessed at work: freedom and autonomy are highly valued and motivational, yet many people are content to be passive and have no real plan. People want responsibility and want to make real decisions yet often are happy enough if the manager just tells them what to do and takes the pressure off. Many people default to victim mentality—it's easier to be miserable and complain rather than charting a course to a better destination and pursuing it with all you have.

As we adopt more positive practices and establish the right conditions for a thriving organization, we help people escape this trap. Weinzweig presents his practices as Natural Laws: "People who are inspired and inspiring are mostly living in synch with the Natural Laws, and the Negative Nellies, Vic the Victims, and Arthur the Autocrats of the world are not."[31] Positive practices like visioning promote a thriving organization. The more we succeeded in living these practices, the fewer Nellies, Vics, and Arthurs we seemed to have at work. And the more joy we find at work without them.

Maybe it's fear—of the unknown, or of being accountable for your own future. Weinzweig continues,

> Visioning for most is unfamiliar, and for many it is—consciously or not—downright frightening. When you're stuck in survival mode, focused mostly on getting by and avoiding what you don't want, it's hard to see that there's a lot more out there to be had if you're willing to vision big. It's so much easier to just lose ourselves in the day-to-day. For most folks, it's much more comfortable to succumb to the status quo of everyday life, even the stresses of success, and get stuck on the treadmills of today, running hard just to stay stuck, than it is to come clear with ourselves about what we really want.[32]

The practices we adopted were aimed at encouraging people to avoid victim mentality and reduce the excuses for inaction. You can't (legitimately) complain about the culture if we clearly explain our values. You can't complain about leadership if we explain what "good" looks like. You can't feel rudderless if we clearly describe where we are and where we're going. And all of these practices can be applied at home as well, creating that virtuous cycle that Ari describes and which is often missing for people at work.

I haven't met many entrepreneurs who were victims. I don't think they last very long. I married into a family of

German entrepreneurs. Victim mentality doesn't go over well with them. Visioning is another means to encourage owner-ship and provide people with training and incentive to take personal responsibility for success. Once a few of us were trained, we came back and created our own version of the training for all employees. It wasn't nearly as good as what we got from Zingerman's, but it was more scalable for our little business. Teaching a practice is a great way to demonstrate you understand it and are commit-ted to it.

> Visioning is another means to encourage ownership and provide people with training and incentive to take personal responsibility for success.

"A vision is a richly detailed and emotionally engaging pic-ture of what success means to us at some point in the future."[33] Zingerman's defined this beau-tifully with that short sentence. Note that it is broad enough to cover an individual, a large organization, or anything in between. That simple description is enough for anyone to get started. And in their training, we got started immediately with the hot pen technique. My colleagues and I thought that this exercise was a little crazy. Before our coffee was cold, we were instructed to go off and write a vision statement. It was a shove into the deep end of the pool—and it worked. It was eerie how many things in our first drafts became reality.

I don't want to delve too deeply into the process of vision-ing here. There are many sources for how to do it, including ZingTrain. My point is that visioning is a positive practice that is critically needed and takes effort to do well. Training people about visioning is the first step: why it's important and the process for creating a vision. This is the easy part. That process is hopeful, forward looking, and unifying. It's like a long, cold drink in the desert. It should lift up and inspire everyone. It's pretty easy to come up with a first draft. It is not easy to come up with one that's ready for primetime. The effort is worth it, because visioning is transformational. Without a vision, you're driving with square wheels.

The really hard part about a vision is clearly communicating it, marketing it, driving it through the entire organization, and keeping the vision in front of everyone. Oh, and don't forget reporting progress transparently and acknowledging the things that didn't get done, as well as the many improvements made along the way. That first draft is lighting the fuse.

Visioning is, eventually, problem solving. Over my career, I've been continually surprised at how many people jump into the solution before agreeing on what the problem is. I've seen an incredible amount of time wasted by teams not clearly defining the problem, and often a lot of effort comes up with a wonderful solution to a problem that we didn't need to solve. An important part of deciding where we want to be is to first agree on where we are.

Bill Burnett and Dave Evans's book *Designing Your Life* had an important impact on me at a critical time. Their views on assessing the current state resonated within my own life: "Deciding which problems to work on may be one of the most important decisions you make." They advise us to beware of "gravity problems"—not real problems because they're not actionable—they are a fact of life like gravity. People fight reality, but you can't outsmart it and you can't bend it to your will. Gravity problems can sometimes be confused with really hard problems that require effort and sacrifice and have a high risk of failure. The only response to gravity problems is acceptance, so this is where all designers begin—start where you are, not where you wish you were or where you hope you are or think you should be—right where you are now. You can't know where you're going until you know where you are.[34]

Some people have a hard time crafting actionable vision statements. Being from New York, I naturally gravitated to what Ari called the *via negativa*—the negative road: *What problems drive me crazy enough today that I really want to solve them in the future?* Harness the power of complaining. Coming up with a clear picture of "where are we?" seemed to be pretty easy when we started with this question. Everyone offered up plenty of things that were wrong in our business. By capturing that dissatisfaction with current problems, we were able to create a clear picture of where we want to be future.

We had to be careful, though, to not let this go too far. We needed to keep coming back to the positives, or we'd turn into Negative Nellies and Vic Victims. Defining problems we don't want to have in the future is not bitching or venting. The current CEO and I recently started working on his vision for the next five years. True to form, we spent a lot of time talking about all the things we didn't accomplish in our last vision. After an uncomfortably long time beating ourselves up, we stopped ourselves and moved to acknowledging all the wonderful things we did accomplish. Starting with the negative might get the juices flowing. Positivity, appreciation, praise and satisfaction needs to fuel the fire for the long haul.

As the picture of where we are becomes clear and we identify all the problems we don't want to have at some point in the future, it can get overwhelming. *My goodness, are we really this screwed up? How are we ever going to solve all these problems in a few years?*

Take heart from this simple phrase: the only time you don't have any problems is when you're dead. Death is not a state most of us are trying to get to quickly. All organizations have problems. If they didn't, they wouldn't need people to help solve them. Don't get overwhelmed. Identify the right problems and prioritize.

> The only time you don't have any problems is when you're dead.

That may sound easy for me to say, and it's a lot easier to write about it than do it. Our leadership team developed individual lists of problems we didn't want to have in the future. Then we stuck Post-it Notes with each problem in the functional area that problem was most connected to. It was easy to see when the same general problem came up over and over. We could then begin to see connections between those problem areas. After a few iterations, we had agreement on our prioritized list. Then our leaders were ready to stress-test that list with their teams.

Visioning means change. By definition, we're describing the problems we don't want to have at some point in the future. We're painting a picture of a place that is different from where we are. We found we needed some training on change management to support our vision. Our favorite resource about that is *Switch* by Chip and Dan Heath.[35] We found the metaphor of the elephant, rider, and path to be helpful in providing our team with a consistent language for change. Here's how I summed up the key premise of *Switch*:

> UVA professor Jonathan Haidt calls the rational part the Rider and the instinctive part the Elephant. The Rider holds the reins and seems to be the leader. But the Rider's control is precarious—anytime the Elephant and the Rider disagree on direction, the Elephant is going to win. Both Elephant and Rider have strengths and crippling weaknesses. For any change to work, you have to find a way to appeal to both and align their interests. And once you align their interests, there's plenty of work you can do to clear the path ahead of them so they can move (change) faster.

In a technology business filled with engineers, we instinctively go for the head—we want the logic and data to appeal to the rider. We don't think about emotions, instinct, and heart. *Switch* helped us realize that we needed to think about reaching the elephant first; if we didn't connect our people emotionally to the change, that elephant was going to go wherever it wanted, no matter how hard we wanted it to go where we wanted it to go.

Here's a simple example of the elephant and rider that you might identify with. Have you ever thought about losing a few pounds? You get excited about that picture in your head of a healthier you. As the rider, you know all the benefits that would bring. Your head is completely committed. Then the elephant smells those delicious French fries, and there's no stopping it. What thoughts are strong enough to overcome the fries? Making a pledge to your loved ones? The thought of being alive long enough to walk your daughter down the aisle or hold your first grandchild? No amount of logic can stand up to the heart, so find the emotion that keeps the elephant on the straight and narrow. When we have the courage to come clear with ourselves about what we really want, that's elephant food.

Switch also helped us think about the path; often the environment for change is ignored as we continue to appeal to logic, data, and reason. The book was full of enough examples that even a bunch of engineers could find a way to reach people's hearts and clear the path by providing the right environment for change to happen.

We also liked Toyota's *kata* system—a process for improving quality through incremental actions. Be sure you agree on where you are and where you are going. Then take a step, see how that works out, adjust, and take another step. Big problems aren't solved with one big solution. Big change is a series of small victories over an extended period of time. This is not one big swing in the bottom of the ninth. It's hours of exhausting, all-out effort by an orchestrated team of professionals. Take steps, ask what's working, look for your bright spots, learn, and craft your next step in the journey. Along the way, publicize the heck out of the small wins and bright spots to give everyone encouragement for the long and sustained effort of change. Celebrate when the change becomes habit.

I wrote the bulk of this book in the summer of 2020 at the height of the COVID pandemic. *Switch* also points out that crisis may be the best way to make change happen. One of my favorite quotes is from Winston Churchill, who said (essentially) "Don't waste a good crisis." And in 2020, we had more than our fair share of crises. If you had told the staff of any major university to move all classwork to virtual classrooms within a week, you would have been laughed out of the room. When we have no choice but to get it done, humans can do incredible things.

> When we have no choice but to get it done, humans can do incredible things.

When crisis hits, most people will see disaster and panic. Leaders should be looking for change that they have been afraid to tackle. Paint a clear and compelling picture of what's on the other side of the crisis, and use the fear and worry to unite the team toward a better place.

In our visioning sessions at Zingerman's, they presented a formula for change that resonated with our group of engineers:

$$D \times V \times F > R$$

Where:

D = dissatisfaction, i.e., the compelling reason to change
V = vision, i.e., the clarity
F = first steps
R = resistance

Crisis will dramatically lower resistance and allow you to make bigger change happen faster. By definition, a crisis means that dissatisfaction with the current state is very high. In a way, if your current state is bad enough, you've got the right environment to enact significant change. This is one reason why I'm hopeful that we will be able to enact more significant changes in racial equity now than we have in two-plus centuries. The recognition and horror created by so many videos of injustice has created broader and deeper dissatisfaction than ever before. If we can only chart the right first steps and paint that compelling picture of the future, we can overcome resistance; not in one big leap, but in a series of steps, adjustments, and more steps.

Visioning is a bit like Values. We need a short and meaningful trigger for the end of the road. Better is a picture or a story that rallies all the elephants around the destination we are heading toward. The ideal is that Roman shield that captures the beauty of our values and higher purpose. Then the hard part is building layers of detail down into and throughout the organization.

With our last vision, we chose five words to mark the main pillars of our vision. In our next vision, we'll likely position the key concepts as Commander's Intent: When the bullets start flying, what's the simple intent of our long-term vision? At its highest level, how does our short description engage everyone's elephant and provide the rallying cry we need to fight the good fight?

Each pillar of our vision had more detail below that, as we did with our values. The pillars can go down to the individual level to capture the key pieces of the vision that you will impact, with detailed plans and goals for the steps you'll take to realize each of the pillars. The detail will likely be easy to create for the first few steps and much more directional for anything beyond a few quarters. That's okay; remember, take a step, see how it goes, and adjust, keeping the end goal in mind. A goal-setting methodology like Objectives and Key Results is great for helping translate the higher level and longer-term aspirations into responsibilities and metrics along the way (see examples in appendix 8).

Obviously, this is a practice that you can employ, no matter where you are in an organization. Even if your company has no use for the hope and direction of a longer-term vision, you can create one for your team or yourself. We found that visioning is unifying. Everyone can participate in the process. Once the picture of the future becomes clear, you can opt in or out—at least you know what you're opting in or out of. The team becomes aligned rather than individuals charting a course that may be in conflict with each other. This is helpful whether it's a group of five or a department of fifty or a church group or a Little League team. The process is the same and the drivers are, as well. The techniques for adopting changes also hold true, no matter what group you're working with. The key driver is taking some control of your own future by painting a vivid picture of what you want that to look like.

Bringing It Home

Visioning is a business practice that's also useful at home. Every parent wants their child to live a better life than they did. We want our children to dream big and take control of their lives. Visioning is a technique that could be adapted for any age. What's the current situation? What are you dissatisfied with now, and what's your vivid picture of the future? What are the key steps you need to take to realize that goal? How do you adapt to unforeseen challenges? What captures your head and your heart enough to put in the long, hard work to get there? How do you celebrate wins? Demonstrating this and practicing together could be one of the best gifts you can give. It could be the difference between a life as a victim on the treadmill and one of joy and satisfaction.

I'm not sure if I made that sound a whole lot easier than it is or if it sounds a whole lot scarier than you thought it would. If this starts to feel overwhelming, too hard, too long—whether personally or in your organization—stop and take a deep breath. Remember that you're headed to a better place than you are at right now. By creating and writing down a clear and compelling vision of the future, you're on the road to a better place, to a better version of you. There will be flashes of success and periods of frustrating "one step forward, two steps back." You won't accomplish every part of your vision on time, every time. No matter what, though, you are better off with a clear vision of where you want to be than you are standing at the fork in the road, waiting for someone to tell you where to go.

> By creating and writing down a clear and compelling vision of the future, you're on the road to a better place, to a better version of you.

TAKEAWAYS

- Visioning is a positive and hopeful practice that helps everyone in the organization. Once learned and practiced, it helps every level of the organization as well as the individuals themselves.
- If you don't know where you're going, it doesn't matter which path you take. Autonomy is one of three intrinsic motivators for people. If you want some control over where you end up, you need to know where you want to be.
- Visioning, like many of the other positive practices we employed, is aimed at encouraging people to avoid victim mentality and reduce the excuses for inaction.
- A vision is a richly detailed and emotionally engaging picture of what success means to us at some point in the future. It's challenging, yet doable. It's a description of the problems that we don't want to have at some point in the future.
- Visioning means change, so executing on a vision requires learning about how to manage change. There are many tools and processes that can help us shrink change. Times of crisis create opportunities, because they reduce resistance to changing the status quo.
- Like values, visioning also requires good marketing and storytelling. It is more difficult to simplify our vision and values to just a few words than it is to come up with a vision. It's also more difficult to drive the vision and values into detailed actions at all levels. That work is worth the effort.

QUESTIONS AND ACTIONS

- From the perspective of your team, what's the most unfair practice in your organization? Why? Now put on your customer hat and ask the same question. How about from the perspective of your other stakeholders? Write a compelling picture of what life would be like without those practices.

- What is your current personal vision? Where are you headed in the next 3–5 years? Why? What problems are you hoping to resolve by the end of this visioning period?

- Have you shared your vision with family and friends? If not, how much more accountable do you think you would be if you openly declared where you want to be? How much more help would you receive along the way if you involved others in your vision?

- In what aspect of your life today are you operating with a victim mentality? Look for things that are frustrating you but where you feel you are helpless to enact change. Think deeply about whether there is some aspect of that problem that is actionable.

CHAPTER 6

SERVICE MENTALITY

*Genuine connections require more
than just a survey score.*

No matter what business you are in, genuine appreciation for the customer must be baked into your organization. That sounds pretty basic, yet we've all experienced companies that view the customer as a necessary evil instead of a critical stakeholder. How do we go about baking the customer into our culture? How do we encourage our colleagues to treat the customer like a stakeholder? How do we identify bad profits? Is there such a thing as a bad customer?

Our value of Service gave us a good start toward creating genuine relationships between our organization and its customers. Service became one of our values, partially because our colleagues developed a deep anxiety about unhappy customers. Like many start-ups, we struggled to get our products right and demonstrate a clear value proposition to attract enough customers to keep us going. Every customer could be the difference between life and death for the company. When we were small, every colleague knew every customer account by name. If anyone was unhappy, we all felt it and responded to it. Once we achieved stability, we kept that deep-seated discomfort about unhappy customers. Eventually, we took this too far and let some customers take advantage of us. We're still adjusting the pendulum swing. With better solutions comes a better appreciation for our value proposition. New colleagues don't arrive with the anxiety of the past and take a more balanced approach. Our Service value was there on the wall throughout our history, and we taught everyone that this value was rooted in customer satisfaction; we don't sleep well when the customer is disappointed.

Service as a value was also the product of being owned by entrepreneurs and closely tied to our ownership-thinking beliefs. Start-ups and entrepreneurs don't seem to lose sight of how important the customer is, because a check from them is the difference between making payroll or not. I heard the story from the founder of a start-up who, in the early days, had to choose between making payroll or paying insurance on his delivery trucks. He chose payroll and kept going by changing the expiration date on all of the insurance cards in his trucks. As companies get bigger, the checks come in, bureaucracy grows, and engagement dims, and it seems a lot easier to forget who pays the bills. We didn't want that to happen.

Despite our history and our values, we struggled to find good metrics for whether our customers were satisfied and what they were really thinking about our offering. We tried surveys early on, when the technology that we have today didn't exist. Those surveys were long, clunky, and hard to rapidly process. Today there are a host of tools available online that make it much easier to create surveys and quickly process results. Instead of clunking along with those surveys, we just kept teaching customer service through our values while searching for something more actionable.

Thankfully, one of our colleagues read about the Net Promoter Score (NPS) in *The Ultimate Question* by Fred Reichheld. From the beginning, it was apparent that Fred was teaching us a positive business practice: "The only way a company can truly live by the Golden Rule—treat others as you would like to be treated—is to avoid bad profits entirely."[36] Bad profits are earned at the expense of the customer relationship. Whenever a customer feels misled, mistreated, ignored, or coerced, then profits from that customer are bad. We've all felt at one point or another that someone we bought from was earning bad profits. It's shameful, and you feel used. We never wanted our customers to feel this way about our business. And we never wanted to send our people home feeling like they did something shameful to line our pockets.

> Whenever a customer feels misled, mistreated, ignored, or coerced, then profits from that customer are bad.

NPS gave us an easy metric that had already been adopted by scores of businesses whose products and services we admired. An NPS survey is straightforward, and there are many resources that make it easy to implement. As you learn about

NPS, the survey and the score are nice metrics, but they're not the end goal. The real goal is to use the metric and the process to magnify the voice of the customer across the entire organization and bake it into the culture. Anything like this that involves the entire organization shouldn't be done halfway. Organizational adoption of change into habit requires long-term commitment. This isn't a date; this is wooing the love of your life. We don't want to launch a fad; we want to stitch a square into the fabric of our organizational quilt.

> We don't want to launch a fad; we want to weave a square into the fabric of our organizational quilt.

Once we recognized that, the ideas flowed more freely. We borrowed an idea from a sister company and included pictures of our customers in presentations and around our offices. We didn't just show the company logo and what they bought from us. We included the person we served, the customer contact whom we dealt with most frequently. People serve people and connect with people much more than with companies. We found our people were often less concerned about pleasing Exxon than they were about pleasing Jane Smith at Exxon.

We do a lot of customer training onsite. This is a great way to expose colleagues to real-live customers. Invite Accounting to sit in for lunch while customers are in the house. Put a real person in front of that entry on the Accounts Receivable ledger—help the customer put similar faces to our company name. Exxon's Accounting department may call our contact to ask about an invoice we sent. If Jane Smith remembers Bill

Brown in our Accounting department, she may get back to her Accounting department a little faster, and we might just get paid a little sooner.

While they are visiting, we ask for feedback. We take quotes from these visits and our NPS surveys and put them on a wall in our biggest gathering spot so everyone can see what our stakeholders are saying about us. We include announcements of our biggest sales wins that tell our team more about the customer and why they chose to deploy our solutions. We look for ways to help connect the sale to our higher purpose: keeping people and the environment safe while delivering the energy we need every day.

Transparency is at the heart of NPS. You cannot sanitize the feedback you hear—you've got to take your medicine. Senior leaders respond personally to follow up on low scores. This brings in another of our values: We CAN handle the Truth. Demonstrating this helps encourage a learning culture and it follows our value of Truth in its entirety. It shows that our leaders can take critical feedback and act on it with care instead of shame and blame. It shows our customers that our values are genuine. It encourages our colleagues to give and receive critical feedback as a path to improvement.

Oh, and the good feedback! I think positive feedback from the customer directly to an individual colleague may be the most impactful and valuable. Our colleagues care deeply about customer satisfaction. What could be better than a customer taking the time to mention your efforts in a survey response that our entire team sees? Recognition and gratitude have even more power when they are specific, so those moments are gold.

NPS can also be turned toward measuring the health of our relationship with another key stakeholder: our colleagues. As Reichheld points out: "The battle to convert customers into promoters can be won *only* if frontline employees are promoters themselves."[37] For years, we surveyed employee satisfaction. Our employee surveys were a lot longer and began to wear out our people. When we went to shorter surveys, we were sure to include the ultimate question: Would you recommend our organization to a friend or colleague? This e-NPS score became a simpler metric to focus on and communicate back to our team. Beyond the metric, though, it helped us face up to our shortcomings and respond to critical feedback like rational adults. It provided another opportunity to demonstrate transparency and continuous improvement.

Eventually, and far too late, we began to build Service and a commitment to the customer into our interviewing process. Other companies do this very well; I recently heard a story about a grocery store staging an interview to present the candidate with a real-world customer service opportunity. During the interview, the company has a mom struggle to load groceries into her car. If the candidate doesn't interrupt the interview to help the customer, they don't go farther in the hiring process. There are plenty of other examples out there. If we don't demonstrate that the customer is an important stakeholder and weave that into all aspects of our business, it is less effective.

Chapter 8 of Reichheld's book is about the importance of hiring, orientation, and culture being important factors.

He writes, "Too many companies kid themselves about their commitment to the customer experience, let alone the Golden Rule. They tolerate great salespeople or great engineers who don't embody the core values of the company. . . . That practice alone tells employees that the values are not the top priority."[38] For NPS to become a cultural service mentality, it has to be woven into our values and a whole host of our practices.

NPS isn't about the score. It's about creating a learning culture that brings us closer to the customer experience. Just like going from employee to manager, when we go from customer to company, sometimes we just seem to forget what it's like to be a customer in our little town. NPS is a process for keeping everyone intimately connected to who is paying our salaries.

As I reviewed our journey about service and the customer experience, I realized that a lot of what we tried to do organizationally was facilitating high-quality connections (HQC) between colleagues and customers. Building high-quality connections is a positive practice that has been studied intensively, and Jane Dutton is an authoritative expert on the practice. "In HQCs, people feel attuned to one another and experience a sense of worth and value. HQCs are critical building blocks for bringing out the best in people and organizations."[39] There are many documented benefits of HQCs.[40] Two of the main pathways to HQCs are respectfully engaging others and building trust. NPS and the practices we

> NPS isn't about the score. It's about creating a learning culture that brings us closer to the customer experience.

adopted in response to Reichheld's *The Ultimate Question* did just that.

Effective listening and supportive communication drive respectful engagement and HQCs. When I asked Jane Dutton about research on the effects of HQC on customer satisfaction, she quickly provided a host of examples. Much of the research is about salespeople. She responded, "Listening demonstrates a sincere form of respect and empathetic concern customer-oriented salespeople have toward their customers. It results in more trusting relationships with customers, better customer satisfaction and loyalty, and improved salesperson performance." Creating HQCs also helps colleagues become more satisfied in their jobs, builds their self-confidence, and helps them become more resilient in the face of unhappy customers. More sales, happier customers, better colleagues—sign me up!

Lots of companies do NPS and do it very well. I didn't promise that the ideas in here were all unique and groundbreaking. After all, I'm really just making sure that my younger self recognizes how important this practice is and understands the dedication required to create the right conditions for it to thrive. Despite all the wonderful technology out there, some companies still don't do this basic thing well. For us, this piece of fabric was made for the quilt of our company. It fit with our values and our culture. It is positive, and there is a wealth of data that shows it to be an essential part of creating a thriving organization that produces results.

What if your company thrives on bad profits and likes it? What if they have their own survey system and you're stuck with it? What if you're running a small department in a big company and you don't want to try to move a mountain right now? What if your department never gets within spitting distance of a customer, ever?

Regardless of the organization, you can still practice the basics of NPS. If you don't have a reason to contact your company's customers, then you must have internal customers. If you can't formally survey enough people to generate an NPS score, you can still informally survey, and you can still work to create high-quality connections between your people and your customers. You don't have to. Many managers don't try. I think you'll see some magic happen when you start to become deeply concerned about your team's customers and you start listening carefully to what they tell you. You'll be demonstrating a learning mindset to your team, and you'll bring more purpose into their jobs. Talk about who your customer is, what they do, and why it's important. Show them the faces and connect them to the people. Listen to them, and maybe even find some training for them on how to listen better. I'm betting that before too long your team will perform better, and everyone might get a little more of that compensation stuff, not to mention a warm glow from the joy of truly serving someone else well.

Bringing It Home

Surveys around our dinner table when I was a kid were pretty simple. Who wants to take out the trash tonight? Who wants to mow the lawn, weed the garden, wash the windows? The scoring was simple: 0 for No, 1 for Yes. Second helpings were available to the 1s. Your family unit is probably not going to survey its customers anytime soon. But maybe you can talk about bad profits and companies that earn them. Maybe you can connect that to your discussions about money. Maybe it's a lesson about fair dealing, the Golden Rule, and the fact that we are all "companies" and "customers" at some point and in some sense. Are we all serving our family unit well? Can we listen more attentively to each other and use these conversations to continue to build the respect and trust that creates high-quality connections at home?

One last quote from Weinzweig on this subject:

> . . . promoters bring good profits to our organi-
> zation. They're aligned with our values. They like
> us, and they like doing business with us . . . they're
> easier to work with for our staff—promoters are in
> a better mood, they're much more patient with us
> when we fall short or make a mistake. The results
> generated by selling to them are more enjoyable to
> get. Which means that the staff's work experience is
> better, which in turn helps reduce turnover, increase
> sales, and makes active promoters out of our staff!
> Again, everyone involved is winning![41]

TAKEAWAYS

- Adopting servant leadership as a core leadership belief makes it easier to bake service into your organization in other ways—like establishing a lasting and genuine respect for the customer.

- NPS is an easy metric for customer satisfaction adopted by scores of thriving businesses. NPS is part of a larger process to magnify the voice of the customer across the entire organization and bake it into the culture.

- Transparency is at the heart of NPS. You cannot sanitize the feedback you hear—you've got to take your medicine. Demonstrating this as an organization helps encourage a learning culture and shows that our leaders can take critical feedback and act on it with care instead of shame and blame.

- NPS is also about building high-quality connections between an organization and its customers. Listening demonstrates a sincere form of respect and empathetic concern. It results in more trusting relationships, better customer satisfaction, more sales, and greater loyalty.

- Building high-quality relationships through respectful listening works at every level and especially at home. Adopting a service mentality demonstrates care and encourages a learning culture; no matter where you are in the organization, there is always something you can learn.

QUESTIONS AND ACTIONS

- Think about your last great customer experience and your last horrible experience. What was the difference between the two? What could you adopt from the good example?

- Where are the bad profits in your organization? What can you do to remove them?

- How is your organization listening to its customers and measuring satisfaction? What are you doing to build long-lasting, high-quality relationships with them?

- Do you approach every situation at work with a service mentality? Do you treat everyone as if they were a valued customer? Try to adopt that practice for a week. Keep a journal and reflect on what life was like when you adopted this approach.

- If you are leading a group or organization, do you remember what it was like to be an employee? In what ways are you staying connected to what it's like to live in your town? In what ways are you working to bring everyone onto the same side of the table to tackle difficult problems together?

PART 2

ACCELERATOR PRACTICES

STRENGTHENING RELATIONSHIPS AND ENGAGEMENT

Mr. Younger Me

Scrappy St.

Hopeful, TX

Re: *Pedal to the Metal*

Dear Mr. Younger:

You have been pre-approved to receive a free set of Accelerator Practices. These practices have been tested and found to be effective in boosting your level of thriving.

Please carefully read the User Manual, as it will help you lower the barriers between you and the rest of the organization. It will help you accelerate relationships and reduce the occurrence of awkward silence and simmering rage.

Also included in this package are tools to deepen engagement, ownership thinking, and teamwork. These practices help pull back the curtain on Oz and bring the full team to bear on a host of issues that I'm sure you are wrestling with largely by yourself.

If you act now, you'll also get practices that increase the level of joy in your organization. Yes, joy: a word that is not associated with organizations enough. This lost emotion may seem anachronistic in today's working environment; sadly, it seems to have been drained from today's working world. Take heart though, as joy is alive and well if you know where to look.

Many if not all of these practices are known and have been

used to achieve success by others. Here, for the first time, you will find all of these packaged up in one offer.

If you act now, within a relatively short time you will begin to see the positive effects on yourself and the rest of your organization.

Kind Regards,

Older You

CHAPTER 7

USER MANUAL

*Trust me, you're going to want to read
this manual cover to cover.*

The User Manual is a short description of how you like to work. How does someone avoid electric shock when working with you? What's important to you at work? What drives you crazy? What makes you happy? Write it down on paper, in bullet point format. Keep it simple and make it easy to read and understand.

When it comes to user manuals, I've found that most people are either like me or my wife. Being an engineer, the first thing I do after I open the box is to read the user manual from cover to cover. (This isn't as difficult as it sounds, because the first thing I do before I open the box is to open a beer.)

My wife takes a different approach. The first thing she does after opening the box is to throw away the user manual. Sometimes she burns it before throwing it away, to be sure it cannot be recovered. As it turns out, her approach works better than mine. Why read a manual when you can watch a YouTube video?

Except that neither approach works very well if there's no manual or video at all. And that's how it is around the office. So, we try to operate each other through trial and error. We just push buttons and turn knobs and see what happens. Sometimes the results are shockingly painful.

I honestly have no idea where I heard about the concept of creating a User Manual for people. Except for obscure sports facts or song lyrics, I'd forget everything—even my own name if it wasn't on my driver's license. And I watched my mom battle Alzheimer's for twelve years like it was the preview for a movie I really didn't want to see. So, if you're reading this and saying, "That's my idea!" please contact me so I can rewrite this chapter and give credit where credit is due.

I had my doubts about the idea of the User Manual until a strange series of encounters with our new VP of Marketing. He would wander into my office and just start talking to me. It usually took me a minute or two to extract myself from what I was doing and focus on what he was saying. He seemed to ramble on in no coherent way about an idea he had or something he was working on. Then he'd stop and look at me for input. I wasn't really following him, so I had nothing to offer. Cue the awkward silence, followed by the abrupt exit, stage left. I began to wonder if we had made a very big hiring mistake. He began to wonder if he had made a big career mistake.

As this scene was being repeated regularly and the tension between us began to build, we decided to try the User Manual concept with our leadership team. The VP and I had a mutual "Aha! moment" once we read each other's User Manuals, and our relationship improved dramatically from that moment on.

Does it drive you mad when people are late to meetings? I worked with someone for twenty years who didn't like to be late and didn't like it when other people were late. But until I read his User Manual, I didn't realize just how *much* he didn't like it when people were late. He took it as a personal affront, like I was telling him to his face how much more important my time was than his. After I read his User Manual, I made it a point to be on time, and our encounters started off on better footing from then on. Talking about this openly also lowered the tension and made it easier for him to give me direct feedback on other topics.

I can think on my feet, but I prefer not to. In the moment, I'm usually thinking first about the smart-ass response. Blame it on my upbringing and too much Bugs Bunny and Abbott and Costello. Of course, I rein that in, and I can add to the dialogue respectfully without preparation. I just prefer to prepare. My User Manual asks that you give me information to digest ahead of time if possible. I'm a pretty good problem solver and, if you give me the situation ahead of time, then I can provide more value than I would in the moment. I'm also better in writing than I am "live," so it helps me think about what I want to say and how I want to say it.

What if you, like our new VP of Marketing, don't know that about me? What I learned about him from his User Manual is that he's the kind of person who likes to work through problems by talking about them. He doesn't like to sit in his office alone and think. He doesn't like to research and analyze until he figures out the broad scope. Of course, he can do those things, he just prefers to talk through things if possible. That unlocks his creativity. His brain is wired to help the puzzle pieces fall into place through talking. What happens when I don't know that about him? What happened with us is a lot of awkward silences, uncomfortable meetings, and probably some hand-wringing around the dinner table until we had our User Manual–induced Aha! moment.

My wife has spent many years training me to be a good husband. The lessons continue. We both hold onto the fervent hope that someday I will be house broken. I try to assure her that day is coming soon.

Maybe you've spent a long time trying to train your manager, or your spouse, or your friend. Relationships are built by working to understand the other person and what makes them tick. It can take years for that to happen. It seems like the days of working someplace for twenty years are gone. Heck, based on the résumés I've seen, five years seems like some kind of record. Even if you're there for ten years, the rest of the cast of characters has changed.

The User Manual is a simple way to accelerate that relationship. Imagine if, on your first day at work, your manager hands you a one-page document that lays down the laws of the land in his little town. Just because I text or email you something on Saturday doesn't mean I want you to answer me on the weekend—I work odd hours and like to capture my thoughts as they come into my head. If you try to play politics with me, it won't end well. Tell me the bad news first. Don't ever throw anyone under the bus, especially not in front of a customer. Don't be late. If you come to me with a problem, I recommend you also bring a solution that we can discuss.

Wouldn't that help you get off on the right foot with your new colleague and stay there? What if you wrote your own User Manual and handed it to your manager? I may be late in the mornings because I take the kids to school and my wife takes them after work so I can work later. I hate to be recognized for my work publicly—it makes me very uncomfortable, so please give me positive feedback in private. I learn best by reading and I absolutely hate public speaking. I tend to take on too many things, so I may need your help prioritizing and saying no to some things. I don't do well without deadlines, so make sure you tell me when you want something.

Wouldn't that help you manage your team better? Wouldn't your team be happier? Wouldn't that save everyone a whole lot of time, worry lines, and gray hair?

I've yet to meet a colleague that didn't want her User Manual to be made public. These are things that people are going to find out eventually. In our experience, people are happy to share their User Manuals with managers and colleagues alike. Nobody works alone anymore. We're all dependent on working across departments at one time or another.

Wouldn't it be nice if you could read someone's User Manual before you met with them for the first time? If you were meeting with a customer, you'd take the time to learn more about them. You'd look on LinkedIn and anywhere else you could look to gain an understanding about that person and what's important to them. Internal customers are important too, yet many people don't take the time to get to know their colleagues. This is especially true in technical fields, where you're more likely to run into a lot of introverts who really don't want to talk at all. Imagine if you knew that lunch hour was sacred for them, or that they really prefer requests for help by email, or they leave at 4:00 p.m. to pick up their kids at school.

Wouldn't it be nice if you could read someone's User Manual before you met with them for the first time?

This is one of the easiest things you can do to improve day-to-day relationships. People have fun doing it. At first, it sounds easy, but many people get stuck. Here's a good question to get you thinking: What drives you bonkers? You complain about it at home, to your colleagues, to anyone that listens, so why not write it down and make the situation better instead of being a victim? Share it with your colleagues and see what they say. Better yet, share it with your spouse or a friend who knows you well. What have you left out?

After we went through this exercise, we had a new manager join our team. On day one, our HR team handed that person the User Manuals for each person on her team. She looked skeptical. What the heck are these things? After reading them and meeting with the team, she couldn't thank our HR team enough. She was the most prepared she's ever been and almost felt like she knew her team before she walked into the room. And my bet is that the team was grateful that they didn't have to work so hard to train another manager.

Our HR team recently took this a step further and

decided to use the User Manual to help find out more about each person's passions, interests, and skills. This helps with job crafting, development, learning, and stronger interpersonal relationships.

If your organization doesn't have this practice, I'm betting that you can implement it without a lot of flak. Call it a team building exercise. If you're nervous about stepping out, talk about the idea with someone in HR—she might want to let you run with it to see where it goes. It doesn't have to take a lot of time. You can start the way you would with a vision document: write DRAFT in big letters and see how people improve on it over time. Have everyone take a crack at it, and exchange the drafts. Discuss over lunch or a social beverage. See if the team comes together just a little more. See if they think you are trainable after all.

Bringing It Home

Work is better when you can be the same person at work and at home. Our people give a lot to our business, and they are compensated fairly for that contribution. But if we can make them better at home, they will be better at work. The User Manual is one of those things that can work at home. Wouldn't you like one for your spouse? Would you read it cover to cover, or would you burn it and bury the ashes? What about one for your kids? (Forget about your mom and dad—it's a scientific fact that you can't parent

> **Work is better when you can be the same person at work and at home.**

your parents.) You may live with someone for twenty years and know something bugs them, but maybe you don't know just how *much* it bugs them. Could this be used to help recognize, develop, and articulate your child's talents?

I also used this practice when I began meeting with a group outside of work. My Work User Manual was okay, but it wasn't personal enough to do the trick in this group. So, I wrote another page of guidance for my personal life. Same guidelines: What's important to you, what drives you crazy? It can jump-start the "get to know you phase" pretty quickly. Though you might not want to use it on a first date unless you're dating an engineer.

In case you get stuck, there are some examples in appendix 3, including mine. Our wonderfully savvy HR Director recently overhauled this form to make it much easier to explore yourself and actively identify the things that are wonderfully, uniquely, you. Whether you use this form or you choose to start with a blank sheet of paper, this practice will help you accelerate thriving.

TAKEAWAYS

- The User Manual is a simple way of accelerating relationship building and eliminating avoidable conflicts in the organization. I've seen it accelerate thriving by improving people's understanding of what makes themselves and their coworkers tick.
- This is a fun exercise that people can knock out pretty

quickly. On one sheet of paper, describe what drives you crazy at work and what energizes you. What are your work rules? What should your coworkers know about you to avoid misunderstandings?

- Check your first draft with a close friend, family member, or spouse—someone who knows you and has already learned how to operate you through trial and error.

- The User Manual is also a great way to accelerate a new manager's understanding of her team and also for the team to accelerate the training process for a new manager. Everyone is happier.

QUESTIONS AND ACTIONS

- Draft your own User Manual for work. See appendix 3 for User Manual examples if you get stuck. Ask a trusted colleague to review it for accuracy, and challenge your colleague to do the same. Did you learn anything new about each other?

- Expand on your User Manual by adding a personal section. Outside of work, what drives you crazy or energizes you? What are your pet peeves and passions? Exchange your personal User Manual with a close friend or loved one.

- As a leader, challenge your team to complete this exercise. Exchange manuals and tell stories about what you've learned. Over the next six months, monitor your team. Did relationships improve? Were you called upon less often to referee conflicts?

CHAPTER 8

OPEN-BOOK FINANCE

Is your team playing the game without
referees, rules, clock, or scoreboard?

I studied finance in business school. I did not study open-book finance. Open-book finance, also known as open-book management, means giving employees all relevant financial information about the company so they can make better decisions. It's a positive business practice used by more than 4,000 companies around the world, including Southwest Airlines, Harley-Davidson, and Whole Foods. "Implementing open-book finance is more than letting employees see the financial statements. When done right, it links financial outcomes with the operations that create the numbers."[42]

I was practicing what turned out to be open-book finance long before I realized there was a name for it. When I became responsible for a business, I wanted my colleagues to feel and act like owners. For me, that started with sharing our financials and helping everyone understand what they mean.

Up until this time, I worked for big corporations: lots of rules, not a lot of mentoring. If you asked for something, you'd be reminded that the company has a strict budget and you probably don't need what you want. These were public companies, so we all saw how the senior leaders were being compensated, and we compared that with our own (opaque) compensation process. We had access to the financial statements but nobody to explain them or connect us to the part we played in them.

As a result, it soon felt like you were playing with other people's money, not your own. It was almost like the company's money was a different color and had a different valuation—one dollar did not equal one dollar. It's like going to Disney World and paying $12.50 for a tiny cup of Kraft° Macaroni and Cheese without a thought. I saw people spend company money like they would never spend their own money, all because it was reimbursed on an expense report. This was clearly a situation where employees were on one side of the table and the company was on the other, with many rules in between to minimize the amount of abuse. To employees, a lifetime of abuse wouldn't equal what the C-suite is making.

Then all of a sudden, I met the enemy, and it was me. How was I going to establish rules to prevent abuse? How was I going to ensure that company money was the same color as employee money? How was I going to encourage my colleagues to treat the business like it was their own? I didn't know where to start, so I started sharing our financial reporting— essentially the same information that management presented to the board of directors.

I quickly learned that most people had never seen financial statements before. The most basic building block of financial reporting is the income statement. This starts with sales, subtracts costs, and ends up with earnings. Businesses that don't care about earnings are usually not around for a very long time. I wanted earnings, and I wanted our team to want them as much as me. I wanted to connect financials to the operations that create them. That meant starting by trying to teach everyone how an income statement worked.

Our early efforts tried to teach our coworkers how the income statement worked by comparing it to your checkbook at home. You were paid a salary, but you didn't get to keep it all. Most parents remember the joyous moment when their child is shocked by how little they got to keep from their minimum wage job. We explained that gross margin equals sales minus costs of goods, like salary minus taxes equals take-home pay. When you look at the salary on your offer letter, you know you don't get that amount in your bank account. When you look at the sales on our income statement, we want you to understand that we've already spent some of those sales to make the product or deliver the service.

We talked about fixed expenses. Rent, utilities, food, and clothing have to be paid for every month. Rent, utilities, salaries, benefits, and a whole lot more have to come out of gross margin every month. We talked about saving up to buy fun things like vacations and big screen TVs. We talked about having to borrow money for big purchases like cars and houses. And how that debt payment absolutely, positively must be paid. We compared those to the big purchases we made in our business and the debt we owed. We talked about how investors expect dividends and returns, just like you want returns from your 401(k) investments.

That analogy was better than nothing, but it never truly clicked with our people. Then I heard a story about a man who owned a small furniture company. One day, he took all of his colleagues out to the loading dock and fired up a chainsaw. He cut an armchair into pieces, then explained what part of sales was represented by each piece. In the end, he held up a four-inch piece of armrest and said, "If we work hard, that's profit." I bet there was some interesting talk around dinner tables that night!

I thought to myself, *We're in the oil and gas business, so let's fire up a blow torch and cut up some pipe!* Thankfully, my team didn't let me near any tools, but we did cut a section of pipe into four pieces that were screwed together. We explained that the whole pipe represented our sales. Almost half of the pipe was labeled "People" and included salary, taxes, benefits—all the direct costs incurred to employ our team. Then there was cost-of-goods, all the rest of our expenses, and finally a small piece that represented profit. It connected people to our income statement like never before and tied back to our purpose. A picture or demonstration is miles better than words. Taking that pipe apart until there was a little piece left put a clear picture in everyone's heads.

I wish I had that prop when we bought another company. We had just closed the deal and were going to meet our new colleagues for the first time. With us were the founders of the business we had just acquired. When we showed them our PowerPoint deck, they were horrified that we were showing employees the income statement. "What's the problem?" I asked. "Well, you're showing them that sales were $5 million last year," he replied. "Again, what's the problem?" "Well, they're going to see that and ask what piece of that five million dollars they are going to get and what we kept."

In fact, the founders didn't get to keep very much at all, and their colleagues seemed to understand all of that just fine. We explained that the solution to the problem was bringing colleagues into the tent and explaining how a business works, not keeping them in the dark. (Or as a friend of mine said a little more crudely, "It's better to have them in the tent pissing out than the other way around.")

Along the way, I read a book called *Ownership Thinking* by Brad Hams. In fact, I was at a Brad Hams conference when I heard about the chainsaw furniture massacre. As I read the book, he really seemed to understand what I had been trying to do. Ownership thinking helps employees think and act like owners toward creating wealth and opportunity while creating a culture that is fun and rewarding. When employees are taught to engage in wealth creation, they become better stewards of wealth and are better equipped to create wealth in their own right.

> When employees are taught to engage in wealth creation, they become better stewards of wealth and are better equipped to create wealth in their own right.

Brad also points out that employees and owners inherently are concerned about different things. He put this into a simple framework that we could use to explain the situation better and work toward getting folks on the same side of the table. He called this moving away from "me-centric" thinking. I call it an exploration of both sides of the table.

WHAT KEEPS OWNERS UP AT NIGHT	WHAT KEEPS EMPLOYEES UP AT NIGHT
Profit: I need to make more than I spend	Paycheck, benefits, health care
Cash: I might have profit but no cash	Job security
Risk: markets, economy, liabilities, contracts	Recognition, reward, career
Competition always making life difficult	Manager, friends, work environment
Finding and keeping good people	Responsibilities, work-life balance

Shortly after I saw this list, I had a meeting with some fellow business owners. One friend was struggling in his business and described his situation as "the constant terror of not being able to make payroll." That is ownership thinking; that is how entrepreneurs and business owners live. How can we help our colleagues understand that feeling without freaking them out?

Brad Hams writes, "What your employees don't know can hurt the company. . . . In the absence of information, people make stuff up."[43] Employees think the company makes wheelbarrows of money. Hams often asks employees how much of sales ends up as profit. A typical answer is 50 percent. That would be ridiculously high for almost every business. This was the situation with the founders of our recent acquisition; they didn't think about providing people with facts to help avoid misconceptions. It never crossed their minds to try to get both management and employees around the table as colleagues.

Hams also correctly points out that people in leadership roles are often uncomfortable acknowledging their lack of financial training and understanding. It helped us realize that nobody taught our leadership team about incomes statements and balance sheets. Those things were shrouded in the mystery of accounting and finance departments. We need to expose them enough to help people understand the rules and the scorecard.

I heard about the book *The Great Game of Business* by Jack Stack from Wayne Baker, a professor at the University of Michigan Ross School of Business who teaches open-book finance. The book tells the story of how open-book finance helped save SRC Holdings, the equipment company based in Springfield, Missouri. The story contains an analogy that I've found very helpful in connecting people to the importance of open-book finance. Working in a business without any knowledge of how the financials work is like playing basketball with no rules, no scoreboard, no clock, and no referees. Basically, you are just milling around on the court with a ball. You might be having fun, you might not. You're not competing or getting better, nor are you passionately engaged. If that sounds a little like your workplace, maybe people need to know more about the business.

A basic understanding of the financials reveals opportunities for us to be on the same side of the table. Health insurance is one such opportunity. Investing time to transparently discuss the costs and alternatives helped us all understand the difficult decisions facing owners. Health insurance and retirement plans are two things that we all belong to and have a stake in, whether you're an employee, owner, or manager. This is one of the most important things to employees and one of the biggest costs in business. We'd be crazy not to openly discuss the cost of the plans and our decision-making process. Our colleagues need to clearly understand what the company contributed, the impact on the business, and how they can help us contain the costs. Invite them into the room where it happens.

As an employee, I took a lot of what the company paid on my behalf for granted. As an owner, I felt those costs. Engaging our colleagues in the costs feels a little like the moment your teenager brings home her first paycheck or pays rent for the first time.

When we do our financial training, we ask our colleagues to guess how much the rent is in the office we're sitting in. That will stop a lot of employees in their tracks. Many don't have any idea. Funny, because the last time we didn't know the rent was when we lived with our parents. As colleagues, we're all aware of what the rent is.

Total compensation statements are another good tool for helping your team understand the business and its associated costs. Many companies have adopted this practice. Instead of just telling a colleague about their salary increase, we provide a statement showing total compensation including salary, bonus, profit sharing, and any other potential payouts like bonuses, commissions, or company car. Then we add in payroll taxes, health benefits, and 401(k) matching. It's eye-opening for most employees to see that salary is less than 80 percent of total compensation. This is what makes the People part of our pipe demonstration so much larger than most people think it should be, and it helps turn employees into colleagues. In the absence of this information, most people think the money is all going to senior leadership and owners.

Colleagues have the data they need to make better decisions about compensation than what they see in a salary survey or hear on the street. They are more connected with the business and its constraints. They are less likely to be surprised by what's happening in the business. Sharing information means the business has a more informed, engaged, and understanding workforce anchored by fact and not the stories around the water cooler.

> Sharing information means the business has a more informed, engaged, and understanding workforce anchored by fact and not the stories around the water cooler.

Our owners are entrepreneurs. They did well more often than not. They worked with their teams to create wealth and value for all. It wasn't difficult to engage them in the principles of open-book finance, including profit sharing. Having a transparent, forward-looking, fair, and meaningful profit-sharing plan helps engage colleagues in the great game of business. Profit sharing is one incentive plan that is very difficult to game and easy for everyone to impact. If you know the basics of the income statement, with a little encouragement you can understand how you can directly impact profit from whatever job you're doing. It adds credence that the business doesn't only serve one stakeholder when profit is shared with colleagues.

Many companies do some form of profit sharing. This might be called an annual performance bonus plan. As outlined in Ham's *Ownership Thinking*, there are simple steps that help make this an engaging practice versus a holiday gift from the owners. The bonus plan needs to be known ahead of time. Maybe that's scary because it becomes a promise, but that's exactly what it should be. People need to understand enough about the financials to understand they can impact the bonus by their individual actions. This is a bonus that we earn together. It reinforces how the business works instead of being a gift from above. I recommend that profit sharing be shared according to a formula that is understood by all and clearly equitable.

If you're not the CEO, you probably don't want to start holding sessions to explain the company's financials or designing a profit-sharing plan at work. You could ask for help in understanding the basics of the company's financial statements (if they are public). You could invite a friend from Accounting or Finance out to ask about the rent or how long it takes to collect money from customers. You could talk with HR about how much the company pays for your benefits and taxes. What facts can you get about the game of business at your workplace? How can you help your colleagues understand the basics of this game within your group? In my experience, walking a little bit in another person's shoes is usually a rewarding experience. If nothing else, a little real information starts circulating to counter the imagination around the water cooler.

> Walking a little bit in another person's shoes is usually a rewarding experience.

Bringing It Home

Many of you may be committed to helping your children understand money. Research shows that continually teaching your kids about money helps them grow up without an oversized fear or desire for money. It helps children make better decisions and become more financially independent faster. This is another area where parenting and managing cross over: helping your people understand how the money works and where it goes will enrich your people and provide a more satisfying experience.

Profit sharing also provides an opportunity for a company to put money where its mouth is on community service and to involve colleagues in giving. In my opinion, a good profit-sharing plan sets aside a meaningful percentage of the pot for community giving. Our Community Service Officer position helped us decide where the money went. Often it ended up as scholarships to a key industry trade association. Or to make an impact in the communities we operate in. Or to a cause that was important to our colleagues. In a good year, maybe all of those. It's another lesson about the great game of business: if you run your business well, you can also create enough wealth to help those less fortunate.

This also applies at home. No matter how much you earn, there are people in greater need. How do we engage our children in the community and instill a sense of giving back to the world? Thankfully, it seems like our children recognize this better than we do and are probably giving us the lessons that we should be giving them. Either way, giving unites and builds relationships. Setting aside something from our bounty is a good habit for business leader and parent alike.

TAKEAWAYS

- Open-book finance is a positive practice used by thousands of thriving organizations. It involves giving employees all relevant financial information so they can make better decisions.
- We found that a simple visual representation of the income statement helped our team get a better sense for how the financials work—akin to a few words for values or vision, the picture is stored in memory and there is a lot more cultural detail and action behind it.
- This is the first practice we've discussed that explicitly is trying to bring management and employees onto

the same side of the table as allies; financial health is a requirement for thriving, and all stakeholders win when the organization is growing and profitable.

- Profit sharing is a great way to engage people in the great game of business. Working someplace without being connected to the financials and understanding how you can impact them is like playing basketball with no scoreboard, clock, rules, or referee.

- Helping your children become financially literate is a lifetime gift. It helps establish a healthy relationship with money, understand the realities of budget, and brings them onto the same side of the table to help.

QUESTIONS AND ACTIONS

- Do you understand your organization's income statement? If you don't, who could help you? Are you willing to be a passive member of the organization without an understanding of how it makes money, now and in the future?

- Look at the table comparing what owners and employees worry about. How connected are you about what keeps the owners up at night? Who could you talk with who could help you understand more about the owner's viewpoint?

- What would be a simple way to explain the basics of the income statement to your team?

- What are a few things that you wish your children would do to help with finances at home? What are some things you could do at work to improve the profitability of your organization? Is there an analogy to profit sharing that you could employ at home?

CHAPTER 9

COMPENSATION PROCESS

Take away the mystery and add
transparency, fairness, and compassion.

SECURITY WARNING—ACCESS DENIED

The website you are attempting to reach:

www.letstalkaboutpay.com

is not secure. Please see your manager if
you want to access this site.

Companies often say that their people are their most valuable asset. Is there any better way to erode the trust of your people than forgetting about the thing they care about deeply?

I clearly remember the day I realized that I was making the same mistake. And I got a dose of my own medicine. It didn't taste very good, but it ended up being good for me—kind of like NyQuil. You see, we care deeply about our people and often tell them how much we value the team's contribution to our success. However, for many years, we stuck with an outdated process for compensation that was not effective and completely opaque to our team. We said our people were valuable, but our actions regarding compensation said otherwise.

In the last chapter, I focused on helping employees understand the view of business. We need to help educate our people on how a business operates so they can be effective partners. Apparently, I needed a little educating myself. I had forgotten what it was like to be an employee. Again.

I had assembled a small group to talk about the 1-2-1 Process and how they could help us implement it. The discussion got heated, and I was facing some challenging questions about why we were asking so much of our team. Out of nowhere, a young colleague from our manufacturing group stood up and said, "Do you even know what an apartment costs in this town?"

In fact, I didn't. Here I was talking about how important it was that our team know what the rent is on our office building, and I didn't know what a one-bedroom apartment costs in my home town. Suddenly, I was walking in someone else's shoes, and they weren't very comfortable.

I was walking in someone else's shoes, and they weren't very comfortable.

We shifted our conversation to compensation and began to build better relationships.

As an employee, I thought about compensation a lot. I had no idea how my employers ever figured out what was fair, and I didn't really think about their problems. I spent most of my time trying to figure out how to get me some more of that compensation stuff. I figured that if I worked hard, did quality work, and wasn't too much trouble, then somebody would recognize that and give me a raise.

If there were any courses about compensation in business school, I was out that day. I frankly don't remember ever discussing anything about compensation until I got a job offer. Looking back, it seems hard to believe that when I left business school I was completely unprepared to handle perhaps the single most important thing to most employees.

For far too long, I didn't really give it a lot of attention once I was in a leadership position. Here I was, finally in charge, able to run my little town how I saw fit after having complained long and loud about the lack of any transparent plan anywhere else I worked, and I didn't try to reinvent it at all for twenty years. I just fell into the routine of doing it the way everyone seemed to do it.

Everyone else seemed to be doing annual performance appraisals, coming up with a rating, and dealing with salary changes on an individual-by-individual annual basis. While we involved employees more in the appraisal process, we didn't establish a transparent and effective process for assessing talent and compensation.

Was I alone in avoiding the compensation process? Did other businesses have the answer and I was in the dark? How did I go so quickly from caring deeply about compensation as an employee to becoming the enemy? Why has compensation become this dirty, taboo subject that company and employee avoid like the plague?

Finally, after we got big enough that the problems with our lack of process were really glaring, we started to do more research, talk to more leaders, and engage our colleagues in the problems.

It was painful to face the frustration I was causing our people by not thinking this through. It was painful to hear about late increases driven by late performance appraisals (that really didn't provide for good decisions in the first place). It was sad to see how much time we wasted apologizing and processing retroactive pay increases because we were so late. It was embarrassing not to be able to answer my colleague's question about rent.

Engaging our team helped me understand how difficult it is to make ends meet with entry-level salary in an expensive place to live. When I graduated from business school, I didn't have enough money left to buy a pizza. I remember standing there at the ATM and trying smaller and smaller withdrawals until I was sure there was nothing in my checking account. No soup for you! However, I had a steady job and everything worked itself out for me. How did I forget what that was like so quickly?

The question about rent reminded me of the frustration behind not understanding how compensation was determined for anyone. We clearly didn't understand enough about the cost of living versus our wages. Our colleagues vented about the perceived gulf between compensation for management versus everyone else. They were understandably looking for answers and expected our leadership to figure this out.

We had open discussions about how difficult it is to

determine a person's worth. Sure, there are salary surveys—those offered data, at least, but the data is flawed. Surveys say nothing about the quality of work life and very little about benefits and specific responsibilities of any given job title. With open-book finance, at least our people knew that half of our sales went to pay for people. I had to convey to the employee what I felt when I became the enemy: the difficult realization that there was no foolproof and completely fair way to determine the price of the biggest cost in our business. People don't arrive with a price tag hanging from their earlobes. We've got some data, and we make the best decision we can afford. Compensation seemed to be a universal problem, and I hadn't met anyone that had it all figured it out.

That dialogue gave us the input and courage we needed to try to address the issue. As it turned out, a big part of the answer was close at hand. A much larger company in our owners' portfolio had adopted a process that was working well for them. We tweaked it to suit our needs, and we ended up with what we felt was a much better solution.

It started by decoupling performance appraisals from compensation. This was driven by several realizations. First, there's no formula we could come up with to fairly go from a performance appraisal to salary increase. That would be an engineer's dream: a formula so elegant that it fairly established compensation across the whole range of variables. Manager assigns a number to performance, establish averages, bell curves, run your formulas, and put people into the right bucket. It happens that way at plenty of profitable companies.

Except, in our experience, that way is inherently flawed

and cannot be fixed. This became completely clear when we asked our colleagues to rate their own performance on a 1–10 scale across each of their areas of responsibility. We did not use that number to determine compensation—we wanted them to honestly assess their own performance as a reflection on what they accomplished and learned over the last year.

The resulting scale bias was clear. [A Google search of "scale bias" or "response bias" reveals a list of research that goes on and on. I don't think we need to dive into that, because we've all lived it.] It always seemed like your friend had the "easy A" manager that worked on an 8–10 scale, while your hard-ass manager worked on a 1–5 scale. When the tables were turned and our colleagues demonstrated their own scale bias, more of us ended up on the same side of the table.

Our head of Finance didn't give herself anything less than a 7. When I raised that observation, she said: "Well, in school a 7 is a C, and I'm better than a C student." Hmm. Didn't you just collapse the 1–10 scale down to a 7–10 scale? Our head of Development didn't give himself anything lower than a 9. His explanation: "At the last place I worked, if you got less than a 9 out of 10, you were fired." Wow—these were two senior leaders in our organization. Apparently, they weren't alone; studies have found that the ratings say more about the rater than the ratee because of these biases and variations.[44] How can we expect the same scale to consistently compare performance across an organization?

Indeed, it seems we can't. CEB (now part of Gartner Group) found that two-thirds of employees who receive the highest scores in a typical performance management system are not actually the organization's highest performers. In addition, only 23 percent of HR personnel are satisfied with their performance evaluation process, and 85 percent have made changes in hopes of improving it.[45]

There's also the issue of the soft skills. We tried to capture that in our performance appraisals for years, because we know the importance of your performance beyond what you deliver. How you deliver is important. On most teams, there are people who may not deliver the most output but are the glue that helps the team perform. Sadly, we've probably all worked with someone that did brilliant work but was an incredible ass. Even if you capture ratings on soft skills, you're still saddled with the scale bias problem.

> There are people who may not deliver the most output but are the glue that helps the team perform.

Another critical problem for us was the limited perspective. If the appraisal is solely based on manager and colleague ratings, we were looking through a very small keyhole at performance. Nobody works in a vacuum. We interact with lots of different people in the organization. Someone may find my soft skills lacking, but another may love working with me. Sadly, your manager may be the most *unqualified* person to assess your contribution.

Sure, it would have been nice to get the additional input from 360-degree feedback appraisals for our people, but we couldn't wrap our heads around the organizational cost. It was burdensome enough to get manager and colleague to assess performance. Multiply that by four to five additional ratings for each person in 360. We were also afraid that some people might game the system by trading good ratings or sabotaging people they didn't like. We find 360 reviews to be useful on a periodic basis or to assess a particular issue or to develop potential. The 360 didn't feel like an annual check-up; in a diagnostic sense, it was more like a colonoscopy (by that I obviously mean something to be done every five years or so).

As we asked more questions and explored the issues, we continued to question the value of the appraisal on its own. Our colleagues and managers begged us not to implement some bell curve–driven increase mechanism. Too many of them had been part of a strong group where team members took turns getting the low increase to satisfy the bell curve while weaker departments got the same money to distribute. I've heard too many stories from people at big corporations that played the game of tag within their department—every year someone had to take the low ranking for the team. The more we thought about it, the more we were convinced that we needed to consider the appraisal as one piece of data in a larger compensation process.

The Talent Review process we deployed worked better than I imagined. Like many other companies, we ended up doing compensation reviews on a set schedule to improve efficiency, rather than leaving it to managers to deal with on the employee's anniversary. We did not want to do all reviews at the same time, fearing that work would stop while every-one talked about comp. Instead, we spread the reviews out by department. Customer comes first, so Sales and Customer Support were reviewed in March. Development was usually driving to key product releases for a Q1 trade show, so they were reviewed in April. Administrative overhead came last in May. Our year is backend-loaded and is filled with year-end close and coming-year planning, so we wanted to get it all done in the first half.

The annual appraisal transitioned into the 1-2-1 Reflection. We have always felt that the appraisal should be driven by the employee and not the manager for three good reasons:

1. The appraisal should be about learning from the past and looking forward.
2. Career and growth should be driven by the employee.
3. The employee is the only one with a front-row seat to everything she accomplished in the last year.

This doesn't mean the manager is not part of the appraisal. It means the discussion moves the two colleagues onto the same side of the table, working on the same opportunity: What did we learn, and how can we grow? We can't do that well unless we honestly assess what happened. It's okay if we have different perspectives, because that drives learning and growth. This isn't about annual feedback because feedback, is an on-going process during the more frequent 1-2-1 Check-ins. The appraisal isn't going to become a number that we're going to feed into the compensation machine. It's not going to be the only determinant of your salary increase. And how you approach the Reflection as a learning opportunity will enter into your compensation—are you genuinely trying to learn and develop?

> We needed to consider the appraisal as one piece of data in a larger compensation process.

The Reflection becomes input for the manager to prepare for Talent Review. The Talent Review provides incentive for colleagues to complete their Reflection and make an honest case for what they contributed over the past year and what they can achieve in the future. A manager can see when you've got data to back up your own rating. Because of our regular 1-2-1 Check-ins, feedback and performance assessment are regularly happening, and both manager and colleague are making notes throughout the year. That becomes the input for the Reflection. In God we trust; everybody else better bring data. The manager is now much better equipped to make a case for each team member. The burden of developing this data is where it should be: on the individual seeking the increase.

> The Talent Review provides incentive for colleagues to complete their Reflection and make an honest case for what they contributed over the past year and what they can achieve in the future.

The manager can now look across her entire team and develop her case for who should get a standard increase and who should not. She is not required to fit increases into a bell curve. She knows that her budget is based on giving everyone the standard, but she has complete freedom to make a case for higher or lower increases for any individual. She may elect to give everyone nothing or recommend that everyone get 15 percent.

But she knows that she has to make her case to a team including her peers, the head of HR, and the CEO. Which means she'd better have good data. She has the freedom to recommend anything and the responsibility to justify it. She knows the budget, the importance of talent, and that half of sales goes to compensation. She cares deeply for her team and wants to do right by them, but they aren't the only stakeholders.

Including a team of reviewers gets us beyond the limited perspective of manager and colleague. The CEO and head of HR are in every review: this demonstrates that compensation is taken seriously. For me, as we grew, my firsthand knowledge of individual performance was very limited, so this review helped me learn more about our people. I didn't have firsthand experience with most colleagues, so I did a lot of listening and coaching. The review team includes peers who would be expected to have valid input. Development might work closely with Sales and Manufacturing but not nearly as much with Admin. You were only in the room if there was a good reason for you to be there.

I was skeptical about this process. I imagined that it would be a political nightmare of alliances between managers and long-standing grudges becoming inflamed. I was wrong. Without a carrot or a stick, managers mostly stayed on budget. Peers offered more positive feedback than negative and were often seen encouraging a manager to give certain individuals more. The manager being reviewed was often surprised by how much their employee was valued by other groups. People had stories about individuals that went beyond numbers.

By design, our leaders care deeply about their people. We've made a lot of mistakes, and often we waited too long to have difficult conversations or take difficult actions. I witnessed many managers who were much harder on another leader's people than they were on their own people. We all have blind spots. Even the best leaders sometimes avoid tackling difficult situations and conversations. The Talent Review became a safe place for us to push each other respectfully. Problems became much more visible, leading to more data being collected and quicker action.

Even the best leaders sometimes avoid tackling difficult situations and conversations.

Feedback was respectful and experiential—there was not a hint of politics. We focused on the exceptions to the standard, high or low. We discussed soft skills. As a group, we made more informed and higher quality decisions about compensation, and we did it efficiently, with input from the people who had the best data. The CEO and head of HR were coaching and asking open-ended questions, not dictating, so we encouraged and supported good data rather than politics and fear.

Along the way, we improved relationships between peers. Our leaders are passionate about their own people and often missed having a respectful venue to talk about people in other departments. The Talent Reviews clearly identified high potential colleagues and engaged the team in developing that potential. Our colleagues could see the time, attention, and commitment of the leadership team to gather good data, run a fair process, and genuinely care.

This process is not groundbreaking. Many other companies have figured out how to do compensation, and probably many of them do it better than we do. Remember that I'm talking to my younger self here, and not necessarily you, my dear reader. If there are any entrepreneurs out there, maybe this helps you adopt a process that is transparent and fair. And maybe somewhere there's someone like me who was out the day we learned about compensation in school.

Speaking of transparent, we collected data on the process and shared it with the team. Increases fell into one of several categories: promotions, above standard, standard, below standard, and sales. The sales team often had very small salary increases and a high percentage of variable compensation. We were able to tell our team the percentage of colleagues in each bucket and the average increase versus the standard. As expected, the majority fell in the standard bucket, and the average increase was close to the standard (duh). We could show people what percentage were above or below and what that meant as well as the aggregate cost versus our budget. This kept us on the same side of the table, looking at the problem of fair compensation while making a good profit. It demonstrated how to measure a process and transparently report on progress.

And we eventually made it back to the question from my colleague that started us down this road. The heartfelt dialogue we had about entry-level pay and the gap between highest and lowest paid made an impression on everyone. We sat down and ran the numbers to see whether we could afford to close the gap and help our lowest paid colleagues.

It turned out that reducing the standard increase for our most senior managers by 0.5 percent would pay for a 2 percent increase in the standard for our lowest paid people. I'm betting that many companies could make that math work.

Rather than being upset, our senior team was happy to cut their increase by a little bit to help raise our lowest wages. They remembered what it was like, at some point in their lives, to live on a shoestring. Maybe they had children who were eking out a living on minimum wage. We look for humble leaders who care deeply about their people, so this wasn't hard to believe.

Even with all that, what happened next was surprising. In our first set of Talent Reviews, managers unconsciously recommended even higher increases for our very lowest paid people. You see, they did the math too, and they could see that a bigger increase had a relatively small impact on budget. They could make a pretty big impact on that person's life without a very big impact on budget. When pushed, they were willing to give up more of their increase to cover more for their people.

So, the next year, we just made this part of the process. Our very lowest paid employees worked from standard +4 percent and the next band worked from standard +2 percent. This doesn't mean they automatically get standard plus 4 percent, it just means that their standard is 4 percent higher. If that person is not performing well, they might not get any increase. They might get more than 4 percent above the standard. A 4 percent boost for someone making $15 an hour is meaningful. And it doesn't take long for that person to enter the next-most-lowest paid group, and soon enough, they would be in the general population.

The leaders whom we wanted were not upset to get lower standard increases. They were compensated well and had performance incentives. It didn't rob from the rich to give to the poor. It wasn't charity or a tax. It wasn't political. It was just the right thing to do in our town.

If you're not the CEO, it might be a lot more difficult to adopt much of this practice. I don't recommend creating your own compensation process in your department and tossing out what leadership and HR are telling you to do.

There are a couple of things you could do. The first is to talk with your HR team. Expect resistance and funny looks. You may not be able to move mountains right off the bat. Building a relationship with HR is a pretty good idea if you are a leader. Talking about what could be done to build a positive organization should help build that relationship. There's not a lot of downside to opening up this discussion as long as it's done with respect and with genuine inquiry. If HR or your manager responds with something like, "Shut up and get back to work," then you know where you stand, and you might be out of luck until you can find a new home. As a CEO, I wanted people to feel ownership for the business and bring good ideas to the table. If the response to raising this issue is painfully negative, maybe you should start thinking about whether this is the right workplace for you.

Even without the blessing of HR, you might be able to engage your peers in a respectful discussion about your people.

Even without the blessing of HR, you might be able to engage your peers in a respectful discussion about your people. I wouldn't call it a 360. It's just lunch or coffee or beer. What interactions do you and your people have with mine? What stories can you tell me? If you were me, what would you be doing to develop your team? This isn't about going around anyone. It's not gossip or a bitch session. It's about collecting better data, even if you cannot use it directly to affect compensation. At worst, I'd be surprised if you didn't get a few specific bits of positive feedback for your team members. More data is usually good, so maybe it will help you build a stronger team, which usually results in getting more of that compensation stuff.

Bringing It Home

How does a transparent compensation process translate to your role as family leader? That depends on what kinds of conversations you're having with your family about money. There are surprisingly few resources out there to guide you in discussions like that. If conversations about compensation are taboo at work, money is probably a difficult can of worms to open at home.

I like practical advice delivered in an entertaining and accessible way. The best book on this topic is Clint Greenleaf's *Beyond the Piggy Bank*. In the beginning of the book, Clint talks about celebrating a success and realizing the potential impact of that on his kids. "While my wife and I wanted to share the rewards of our hard work with them, if we didn't give them the context . . . we would raise kids who expected to be given opportunities and rewards instead of working to achieve them."[46] I feel like most parents have a fear of raising kids who turn out to be entitled brats. Going back to the CEO viewpoint, working in a culture of entitled adult brats is really no fun at all.

This is not to say it's easy. Parenting is already a tough road, even before COVID-19. Teaching your kids (and maybe yourself) about financial literacy is quite a bit harder than enjoying an adult beverage while watching reruns of *Law & Order*. This is one of those "pay me now or pay me later" moments. Dealing with the aftermath of not dealing with it is more painful than dealing with it, just like teaching financial literacy and open-book finance is a good investment as a business leader.

As Greenleaf points out: "Financial literacy rates are at an all-time low. . . . The percentage of high school students who pass financial literacy tests stands at 7 percent."[47] And don't think you're getting help at school:

> As of 2020, only 21 states require students to take a course in personal finance. . . . The best place to start is to explore your own financial values and assess your own level of financial literacy. . . . Since each person and family has different values, it's good to examine how your bigger personal values relate to money.[48]

Leaders tackle difficult and uncomfortable issues that impact the people in their care. It's imperative that they do. There are resources out there to help, whether it's tackling compensation at work and reducing the discomfort of those discussions or it's laying the groundwork for your child to have a healthy relationship with

Most things that are worthwhile and impactful will require sustained effort.

money. Yes, it's hard. Most things that are worthwhile and impactful will require sustained effort. Knowing that you can make your own town a little better can give you the motivation and energy to tackle the tough issues.

TAKEAWAYS

- A transparent, fair, and thoughtful process for assessing talent and determining compensation helps remove the mystery and engage the team as allies working to ensure equity. An organization cannot thrive unless this challenge is faced and addressed.

- Compensation is perhaps the most important aspect of the relationship between organization and employee—it is almost always the organization's greatest cost and is obviously critical to the employee. Yet there don't seem to be many good models out there for a good compensation process, and it remains a mystery to many employees.

- Somehow management forgets what it's like to be an employee once they face the realities of budgets (and are very well compensated themselves). Employees are not often connected enough to the financials of the business and don't understand how difficult it is to set fair compensation. A good first step is to engage in respectful dialogue about the subject and understand the challenge. Leaders tackle difficult and uncomfortable issues that impact the people in their care.

- Because of scale bias, a direct link between a manager's appraisal and compensation cannot be fair. We transformed the appraisal into a reflection focused on learning and improving. The compensation review included broader viewpoints of individual contribution, to be more fair.
- Our leaders also gladly reduced their own standard merit increase in order to pay for higher merit increases for the lowest paid positions in an effort to reduce income disparity.

QUESTIONS AND ACTIONS

- How much are you worth at work? How do you know that?

- If you were given the freedom to set the compensation for each of your coworkers, how would you go about doing that fairly?

- How much does a decent apartment cost in your town? How much is the monthly rent on your office building? Sit down with your team and ask both of those questions. What was the most striking thing about the answers?

- Ask each of your team members to assess their own performance on a scale of one to ten. Do the same with your own performance.

Now assume that your next salary increase will depend on that assessment. Does your score change?

- How do you establish a fair allowance for your children? Did you explain how you arrived at that figure? How might an open conversation about this set them up for a healthier understanding of compensation in the working world?

CHAPTER 10

CULTURE COUNCIL

Free resources, mistake insurance, engagement,
communication . . . what's not to like?

One of the most painful experiences I had was when four-teen of fifteen people in the same group all quit within a five-month span. Thankfully, the loss of this group was not fatal to our company. It was certainly a meaningful amount of our sales: we had customers who counted on us, and we had rent to pay. However, it wasn't the financial impact that was so painful. The painful lesson was about losing touch with a group of remote employees and the betrayal of the trust we placed in their leader. In the end, it turned out that leader was having a completely different conversation with us than he was having with the people who reported to him.

I trusted him, and so did his manager. All appearances led us to believe that he was capable, honest, caring, and com-patible with our culture. We were wrong. Unfortunately, his people also thought he was honest and caring. They believed him because he was closer to them. He worked with them all the time. As "management" working from headquarters, we did not. We misread the entire situation, and we didn't stay close enough to what it was like to be them. We thought that employee surveys, open-door policy, and a good overall culture would help us stay in tune with what our team really thought about our business. Those things helped a lot, but they didn't save us in this case.

The painful lesson I learned is that the most dangerous people are the ones who are very good at appearing to be decent, caring and honest. I can deal with all manner of issues if I can accurately assess what the issue is. It's the looping left hook that comes out of nowhere that knocks me out. Growing up in New York, I prided myself on have good street sense and believing that everyone is dishonest until proven otherwise. To this day, I wonder what we could have reasonably done to prevent what happened. In a culture built on trust, how do we protect ourselves from abuse? I realized that this is part of the baggage that management and businesses are carrying around.

> The most dangerous people are the ones who are very good at appearing to be decent, caring and honest.

Trust is at the heart of every good relationship. We have many relationships throughout our lives, and their value is measured by mutual trust. Unfortunately, our working relationships are often sorely lacking in trust. Transparency and truth are the foundation of trust. We build trust over time by revealing ourselves and speaking the truth. Often it takes years to build trust. Companies are not traditionally transparent, and managers don't often unveil their true selves or their motivations. The working relationship becomes a poker game, a negotiation that depends upon concealing facts and feelings in hopes of winning the game. Imagine if our personal relationships operated like our work relationships. Zero-sum games do not create lasting happiness.

As an employee, I spent my fair share of time commiserating with my coworkers about management. We second-guessed decisions that didn't make sense and were not explained. We wondered aloud about many events, and we made up for real information by inventing our own theories that quickly became facts, at least in our eyes. Nobody really explained what went on behind the curtain in Oz. We got the smoke and the mirrors, lightning and thunder, policy and procedure, negotiations and love songs. We didn't get a glimpse into the inner workings of the machine. That was reserved for management.

Zero-sum games do not create lasting happiness.

Then one day, I became the enemy. I was the company and management. And I quickly became painfully aware of why many companies are not completely transparent. I experienced the reasons why companies and managers are reticent about truth and trust.

Our Culture Council helped create trust by uniting both sides of the employment relationship as colleagues. It helped me avoid many mistakes as CEO. It is easy to become entrenched in your own view and be blissfully unaware of what others feel or think. We all need more listening and less

We all need more listening and less preaching.

preaching. As the saying goes, before you judge someone, walk a mile in his shoes. I had walked miles as an employee and as management, yet I was forgetting what those employee shoes felt like. It's easy for a CEO to live in a bubble and lose sight of what it's like to be a citizen in his town. The Council (or Counsel, if you like double meanings) helped me make sure I was better connected.

Our Council is a subset of about 5 percent of our employees who regularly meet with the CEO and head of HR to openly discuss the business. This was very easy to do and only required a small investment of time by all participants. The payback made that investment a winner for all concerned.

Membership is voluntary. We make it clear that this "second job" is not a forced march, and declining an invitation to join or asking to leave would have no impact on career, compensation, or standing. Whether people completely believe that or not I cannot say, but I can honestly say that we genuinely operate that way. We purposefully do not hype membership in the Council or promote it internally or externally. We want this to be a working group of equals who are genuinely concerned with making good decisions about the workplace and our culture.

It is important to have membership that cuts across work experience and departmental lines to provide a diverse and broad set of perspectives. We invite people who seem

to understand and support our culture, but we also invite a few people who openly oppose management. We found that naysayers often provide interesting viewpoints that challenge our percep-
tions. In rare cases, those naysayers became raving fans because we listened respectfully and took the time to explain our thinking. At worst, the naysayers became noticeably less vocal when exposed to an alternate reality, or they decided to leave because they found it harder to complain when they had a hand in how things were managed.

> Naysayers often provide interesting viewpoints that challenge our perceptions.

We do not allow managers to become members of the Council. If you become a manager, you leave the Council. This happened more often as we realized that the Council uncovered a few high-potential colleagues. Council meetings gave us an opportunity to see how people approached difficult decisions, sticky policy issues, and the process of balancing the needs of all stakeholders.

The CEO and head of HR treat the Council like an internal board of directors. We provide necessary background materials before meetings, and we share the agenda in advance. We solicit the Council for additional topics of interest. We share progress reports and are accountable for actions taken or deferred.

The Council gives us the opportunity to vet ideas, policies, and decisions before announcing them to all of our colleagues. It provides us the opportunity to hone our thinking and messaging to our audience, and it allowed us to avoid many missteps that could have cost considerable time and emotional currency.

The Council also helped magnify my voice with all colleagues. There are many issues, decisions, and discussions that are not effective in an all-hands meeting, town hall, or company-wide communication. It is more difficult and time consuming for the CEO to visit with colleagues in small groups across the business. By meeting with the Council, I was assured of having at least one voice within departments that could counter the alternative truths being developed around the water cooler.

It is much easier to survey colleagues and customers than ever before. However, that technology has created survey fatigue. And oftentimes, issues are complex enough to require more background than a survey allows. We equip our Council members with the background information they need to do informal surveys. Our colleagues receive these requests as peer-to-peer dialogue versus yet another company request. Our best Council members survey their colleagues about upcoming agenda items and arrive at meetings prepared to provide broader feedback.

Our Council members value the opportunity to influence decisions and clarify communications. They enjoy being brought behind the curtain to learn how the machine operates. Just as I learned when I became the enemy, our council members realize that seemingly simple issues were often much more complex and difficult to resolve fairly. They learn that our laws often prevent managers and company from explaining the backstory, leaving the company unable to defend itself to some of its most important stakeholders. They develop a better understanding of the great game of business while helping management understand what life is really like in our little town.

Over time, the individual dynamics of the Council shifts with its membership, yet it remains a place where respectful disagreement is welcome, and it creates a valuable bridge that unites employees and company as colleagues. It helps build the trust that is so necessary in any productive relationship. The Council helped lower the barriers between management and employees and reduced the risk of that sweeping left hook out of nowhere.

The book *Humble Inquiry* by Edgar Schein is a good read for any leader looking to improve the free flow of honest communication. Schein writes:

> What we have to learn…is how to bridge those status gaps when we are in fact mutually dependent on each other. It will be easy for the subordinate to continue to be humble and ask for help of the superior. The dilemma that will require new learning is how the superior can learn to ask for help from the subordinate.[49]

We build trusting relationships by asking more than telling and by showing a genuine interest in others.

We were conducting our annual employee survey when we lost virtually that entire department over the course of a few months. All of the people that left us replied to the survey, but we didn't have all the results ready to present until many of them were gone. As our part-time Chief People Officer, one of my jobs was to help analyze the survey results and report back to our colleagues. My first instinct was to exclude the results of that entire group. Obviously, they were being led down a road that was not based in fact. The ratings from that group were significantly lower than any other group in our company. My engineer brain kicked in and started complaining

We build trusting relationships by asking more than telling and by showing a genuine interest in others.

about that data being tainted. I should have realized that I was really just trying to avoid reporting those results. The wound was fresh, and I was rationalizing. The Culture Council called me on it and helped me avoid visibly going against our value of Truth. They reminded me that Truth was about facing the uncomfortable moments in our lives and carefully considering what they are telling us about how we can be better.

Thankfully, I listened to them better than I listened to Mom, and we presented the full results in all their messy glory. We accepted responsibility for losing touch with that team. Over time, one or two of them came back to work with us. Eventually, we rebuilt the group and got sales back to where they were before. If not for the Culture Council, we might have done more lasting damage to our culture by failing to live our values at a difficult time. And we decided to make sure we had representatives of our remote sites on our Council, to stay a little more in tune with what it's like to live in our town.

As the COVID-19 crisis hit, we turned to the Council early and often. We needed to understand what people were most concerned about and what they were dealing with. We needed to help them understand what the rest of our stakeholders were thinking and feeling. Through this dialogue, we recognized that people were understandably worried about their jobs. We were able to pose to them a question that we faced: Would our team rather take pay cuts if things got bad, or would they prefer limited layoffs or furloughs? Our culture came through—as colleagues, we would rather see pay cuts than put someone out of a job at a time of crisis.

This led us to develop financial plans built on escalating pay cuts driven by different levels of sales results. Demonstrating servant leadership, our leaders took the first and deepest pay cuts. We worked with the Council to communicate the plan so people knew what was coming as the crisis unfolded. Our new HR Manager, who started just days before the stay-at-home orders, was unsure. She had not seen this level of transparency before and was more than a little curious to see how it would play out. Six months later, she credits this transparency, and our long investment in culture, supported by the Council, for helping us all come together and weather the storm better than she thought possible. Working together as colleagues on the crisis made it more manageable.

The Council saved us from many more mistakes. We worked together as colleagues to honor the values that form the foundation of our culture. As colleagues, we all have a vested interest in creating a thriving workplace. In turn, our Council members learned more about the great game of business and became leaders by accepting responsibility for others. They became active guardians of our culture and builders of our society. They helped improve communications throughout our business by quashing rumors with facts. Imagine if Congress and the President could come together in a similar way, as engaged and respectful colleagues genuinely honoring our values, strengthening our culture, and helping to ensure a thriving organization for everyone.

What are the lessons here for your town? I think most managers instinctively establish closer relationships with a subset of their team. These "lieutenants" become the leader's culture council and help keep her connected to what's happening with the team. Like our Culture Council, for this to work positively, the communication must be genuine and two-way. If this becomes part of a command-control strategy, it is far from a positive technique to break down walls and keep you connected. If it is solely within your team, it can also be insular—drinking your own bath water isn't healthy. It's not healthy if your council is a group of yes-men. Your advisory should feel comfortable calling you to task, disagreeing with you respectfully, and helping you appreciate their perspective. Maybe you include a naysayer on your council. Maybe you include people who work with your team but don't report to you. Anyone that can give you a broader perspective on what life is really like in your town might be a good person to have on your council.

It's not healthy if your council is a group of yes-men.

Bringing It Home

As a parent, I think many of us feel and act like home is the one place where we really get to call the shots. We might have felt powerless as children, then as students, and likely again at the office. Often there is not a long history of transparency, vulnerability, and autonomy along our paths in life. That's one reason why most of us have had managers who led from a position of power instead of a mindset of service. They drive us crazy at work because we're told what to do, second-guessed, and spoon-fed information. Frustrated, we arrive home looking to exert control. And we repeat with our children what we experience at work. Hopefully that bleak picture is not your story. Culture Council created opportunities for honest feedback and helped others understand the company's perspective so we could engage them as partners in achievement. Why wouldn't that work at home?

TAKEAWAYS

- A good advisory council can help leaders avoid mistakes, deliver clear messages, and stay connected to what life is like in their town. At the same time, it helps develop leaders and engages more people in the management of the organization.
- An advisory council should be diverse. It should include as many different viewpoints as you can assemble in a group of ten or twenty people. While it should largely include team members who understand and support the culture, it should also include some colleagues who are clearly not satisfied with how the organization operates.

- As the organization grows, it is easy to lose touch with stakeholders. A good employee advisory council is an efficient and effective way of staying connected to what life's like in your town. It also brings employees onto the same side of the table to resolve organizational issues collectively.
- The leader must exercise humble inquiry and do more listening than talking. The leader should treat her advisory council with the same respect as she would her board or manager, in order to build an effective council.

QUESTIONS AND ACTIONS

- Think about the mistakes you've made in your career. Are there any that you could have avoided if you have been able to quickly survey the pulse of your organization?

- Who will you invite to your own advisory council? What does each bring to the table? Does anyone on your advisory make you uncomfortable or challenge your views?

- Do you run your family from a position of power, or do you seek to bring everyone onto the same side of the table? Is everyone's opinion heard and respected?

CHAPTER 11

SECOND JOBS

*Believe it or not, some of us are happy to
take on more responsibility for free.*

Culture Council is an example of giving colleagues second (unpaid) jobs within the organization. Many employees get unpaid second jobs at work—just not voluntarily. Most second jobs are just additional responsibilities that are assigned without a thought about whether that colleague is suited to the task or has the bandwidth to take it on. You might have missed a meeting and found yourself with one of those unpaid second jobs.

The second job that I'm speaking about is one that taps into an individual's passion and talent. These jobs are completely voluntary and require no coercion or threats. Imagine asking an employee to take on an additional responsibility for the company without additional compensation and being met with enthusiasm, joy, and exceptional performance. If I had not seen it with my own eyes, I would not have believed it was possible.

All too often, the working relationship is devoid of personal interests. Good managers realize that genuinely caring about their people as individuals is critical to building a successful working relationship. Unfortunately, many managers are unaware of what is important to their colleagues outside of work unless there is a crisis, and then they sometimes feel like they are dragged unwillingly into someone else's personal life. Many managers spend their time focused on what an employee doesn't do well rather than figuring out what makes that person uniquely wonderful.

Marcus Buckingham and Curt Coffman's book *First, Break All the Rules* influenced my leadership and growth by encouraging me to focus more on people's talents and positives rather than trying to fix their weaknesses. They point out that one of the signs of a great manager is the ability to describe in detail the unique talents of each employee. Great managers see themselves as catalysts and try to figure out better and better

Focus more on people's talents and positives rather than trying to fix their weaknesses.

ways to unleash employees' distinct talents. They try to carve out unique expectations and measure outcomes. They try to highlight and perfect talents.

As managers and company become more informed about the people working within the organization, they demonstrate that they care and put action behind phrases like "Our people are our most important asset." Like everything else in a healthy relationship, this must be genuine—caring about people for your own benefit is bound to fail.

As James Robbins writes in his book *Nine Minutes on Monday*: We like to know we are cared about and we hate being used. We all love people who don't want anything from us but rather want the best for us. "The simplest way to show you care is by taking a genuine interest in their lives... Take it slow and make it genuine".[50]

> As we get to know our colleagues' individual skills, talents, and passions, we can often find opportunities for them to help the organization doing something they love.

As we get to know our colleagues' individual skills, talents, and passions, we can often find opportunities for them to help the organization doing something they love. This is a win-win instead of an edict that is resented.

A good example of how this worked is our 401(k) investment committee. Retirement plans require regular meetings of the investment committee for oversight and decisions about investments. These meetings usually include the CEO and the CFO or head of Finance. This is a serious responsibility, because the committee members have a fiduciary duty to help manage the retirement plan for their fellow employees. As a result, this feels like an unpaid chore to some people, and they arrive unprepared and grumpy. Of course, I'm not speaking from personal experience.

Okay, yes I am. As soon as I heard about the concept of second jobs, I thought about finding someone who would willingly replace me on the 401(k) committee. We sent a note around to our team asking for employee representation. I honestly didn't think anyone would respond. Pretty quickly we found two volunteers who love investing. In their spare time, they follow the markets and think a lot about returns and asset allocations. This was wonderful, because this money belongs to all of us, and good oversight is important for everyone in the plan.

These individuals love being on the committee. They arrive more prepared than anyone else and they ask great questions. They understand that they are providing an important service to their colleagues and are driven by the satisfaction of helping others. In so doing, they become an extension of our HR team as it related to 401(k)—they understand our plan better than almost anyone. When changes are made and communicated by our plan provider (typically in a form letter), our employee representatives take the time to answer questions and explain decisions to their colleagues. In short, they get to do more of what they love *and* help people they care about.

After that, we started looking for other second job opportunities. Our marketing team discovered two colleagues with a passion for making videos. One of our IT support people flew drones and had his own high-end video equipment. A software manager owned expensive video editing equipment and loved to create finished product. Together, the team created genuinely wonderful videos for our company at a fraction of the price we would have paid an outside firm. They loved doing it, and the Marketing team was happy to avoid explaining our business and culture to outsiders.

Responsibility for social consciousness is often set in the lap of HR or Marketing. Often this creates an undue burden on overworked individuals. We created the position of Community Service Officer and solicited volunteers to help. This was sometimes an individual, sometimes a small team, but always volunteers with a passion for community service. We entrusted them with handling applications for matching grants from our colleagues and deciding on scholarships we offered from part of our profit-sharing plan. They were the ones holding the big check when we made our annual donation to the food bank. It was a lot of work for no more pay than the satisfaction of encouraging others to give to those less fortunate and the joy of seeing the faces of the people they helped.

The establishment of the CSO position resulted in an unsolicited team of volunteers seeking to help our business be more environmentally conscious. We were too small to afford a full-time position to do this. We weren't a consumer products business worried about what our customers would think if we weren't thinking about the environment. Regardless of whether our customers cared, some of our other stakeholders cared a lot. The only way we could justify the effort was to do it with volunteers. And thankfully we had plenty of people who were passionate about doing our part to help the planet. Soon enough, the self-named Tree Frogs had recycling bins everywhere and found a program that improved our lighting systems and lowered our energy bills.

Another team of volunteers helped organize physical fitness classes at lunch and after work. This group worked with HR to find fun events and make sure people were aware of the rewards available if they found time to take care of themselves. It was particularly satisfying when our colleagues took it upon themselves to bring their passions to work and help the greater good.

It seems like a business never has as many resources as it would like to be great. Budgets are always constrained. These teams didn't work perfectly all of the time. People didn't always have time to put their passions to work in second jobs at work. Sometimes people volunteered for the wrong reasons or they didn't realize the workload they would be taking on. Despite the imperfections, there was a lot of success. I want Younger Me to be looking for ways to learn about our colleagues' personal passions and to give them the opportunity to use their strengths to help our business by doing the things they love.

And I suppose those opportunities exist in any group or organization. How many churches know the best volunteers for the bake sale? Volunteer organizations seem to understand this completely, maybe out of necessity, because they never have enough money to make ends meet. Necessity drives invention and creativity, so somehow the most strapped organizations take the time to get to know their colleagues and find a way to employ their passions to help the organization. While "free resources" are good for the organization, it's only half the benefit. People don't experience enough joy at work. They don't get enough of the positive feedback that builds confidence and resilience. They don't get enough opportunities to shine as a uniquely talented individual. Too many places create environments where people can't bring their true selves to work. Too many people feel like anonymous cogs turning in the big machine. Second jobs provide an unexpected shot of joy and confidence for those who step in and reveal their passions.

Bringing It Home

I think we do this in families too, though maybe not intentionally. I had a lot of second and third jobs when I was growing up, but I'm not sure my mom and dad gave those to me because I had a passion for weeding or a special talent for mowing the grass so it looks like Yankee Stadium. I am sure that my daughters (and really any grandchild) have lifetime jobs as Tech Support for their parents and grandparents. I have one brother-in-law who can tell you anything about skiing, and another is an expert on innovations in education. My sister-in-law is the guardian of relationships. You see pride and energy when you see them practicing what they love. Many families do this naturally, as humans have likely been doing since the caveman days. I can't cite much research from prehistoric times, but I can tell you that discovering and applying personal passions can magnify your impact without additional investment in resources.

There are a couple of practices in here that can be used to facilitate the search for passions and talents. Our team just revamped the User Manual **Helping someone** to help with this, and the Position **discover their** Alignment is geared to seeking out **talents is a gift** talents. It's not easy, it doesn't hap- **that makes leaders** pen overnight. Many people haven't **and organizations** thought much about their talents **memorable.** and passions. Drawing that out of them provides yet another benefit to everyone. Helping someone discover their talents is a gift that makes leaders and organizations memorable.

TAKEAWAYS

- Second jobs tap into talent and passion to magnify resources and fill organizational holes while also helping to identify individual talents, boost confidence, and create joy.

- Great leaders look to discover the hidden talents of team members and develop them. Often those talents can be employed in new ways to help the organization while increasing an employee's engagement at the same time.

- Second job ideas are almost as plentiful as individual talents. Ideas include an employee advisory, environmental sustainability, DEI, marketing, 401k oversight, and community engagement.

- One of the great gifts a parent can bestow on a child is to help uncover talents. This is also true for spouses, friends, and other family members. Many people go through life without recognizing their gifts, and all too often our society focuses on what is left out of someone.

QUESTIONS AND ACTIONS

- What are your passions outside of work? Is there any way you could apply those to help the team at work? What are your coworkers' passions outside of work?

- How well do you understand your team's innate strengths and personal passions? Consider employing the User Manual to begin to uncover those strengths. Delve into the Position Alignment to identify why they love to spend time on certain activities. Tell each member what you find.

- The next time you find yourself frustrated about what someone else is not doing well, stop for a moment and focus on what that person does that is wonderful. Are you spending too much time trying to add what you see as left out of that person rather than the gifts that are already there?

CHAPTER 12

GRATITUDE

Saying thank-you a lot means never having to say you're sorry.

*Note to Self:
Thank someone
today! You'll feel
better and so will
they — win/win!*

Adam Grant writes, "A sense of appreciation is the single most sustainable motivator at work. . . . Your raise in pay feels like your just due, your bonus gets spent, your new title doesn't sound so important once you have it. But the sense that other people appreciate what you do sticks with you."[51]

In a study including over 200,000 participants,

"appreciation for your work" was ranked as the number one factor for happiness; work-life balance was number three, career development was number six, and salary was number eight.[52] Even after adjusting for age and nationality, appreciation consistently ranked as the single most important job element for all participants. Yet in a 2013 survey of 2,000 workers, 80 percent agreed that receiving gratitude makes them work harder, but only 10 percent expressed gratitude to others every day.[53]

When recognition happens regularly, people will stay longer and deliver increasingly better results. Employees who are appreciated are less likely to keep asking for more salary. Professor Kim Cameron at the University of Michigan has studied the impact of virtuous practices including gratitude. "Frequent and sincere expressions of appreciation have been found to produce dramatic effects on individuals and organizations."[54] In a study of thirty health care organizations, frequent expressions of gratitude were strong predictors of patient satisfaction, employee engagement, and turnover. Show genuine appreciation and it will produce great results—for customers and for employees—in the workplace and at home.

The role of gratitude and recognition in creating a thriving workplace is indeed well documented. Even without diving into the research, the way Adrian Gostick and Chester Elton put it in their book *The 24-Carrot Manager* is pretty compelling: Unless we truly value our people, we cannot

Valuing people = happier customers = more profit.

effectively serve our customers. The most hardhearted manager can follow the logic: valuing people = happier customers = more profit.

Traditional thinking about recognition leads us to carrot and stick. And carrot typically means money. So many managers pitched a financial incentive plan to me over the years that I finally put a warning about it in my User Manual. Daniel Pink's excellent book *Drive* became a cornerstone of our leadership training. What I found during my career convinced me that monetary recognition is a very dangerous weapon, to be used only by experts for specific and limited needs. Cash incentive plans are not over-the-counter medication and should be labeled "Use only as directed."

One type of financial reward that I can get behind is meaningful service awards. Handwritten notes and plaques are appropriate for less than five years of service. Decades of service are increasingly rare and warrant a meaningful cash bonus along with a plaque. We included service awards in our company meetings to celebrate the achievement and express our appreciation. Our division leaders were adept at recognizing each individual's positive traits and contributions.

As a manager, our worst days are when a valued colleague hands in their resignation without warning. We worked so hard to find and train that person, and we count on them for so many things. The thought of going back into the market to find a replacement turns our stomachs. Yet we often don't do simple things as an organization to help improve retention. Couple meaningful service awards with a "stay interview" (what keeps you here), and you have demonstrated appreciation and respect for that colleague's loyalty and devotion.

Referral bonuses are another financial thank-you that is simple to do. Our best hires came as referrals from our colleagues. We operate in a very competitive market for talent. Referrals already understand a good deal about our culture and are an immediate fit. They arrive with at least one friend at the office. They know a little about our products and our customers. They come up the curve faster and stay longer. Given how important it is to find good people who fit our culture, it seems like a no-brainer to provide a meaningful financial incentive to a colleague who helps us find great employees.

Referrals don't apply just to bringing talent in from the outside. Leaders have a responsibility to develop talent, even if it means their life is more difficult. It's my job as a leader to think about where my people can go next to grow. I have a responsibility to provide honest referrals about talent. A good talent review process helps encourage this behavior and helps managers see when they are holding someone back. One of the best ways you can recognize your people is by letting them go.

How do you recognize people without money? One of my favorite ideas sounded great, but in practice it didn't work. The idea is that whenever you welcome a member to your team, tell them: "I know you are going to do great things and we will want to recognize you. How do you like to be recognized?" I thought that was a great way to learn how to deliver praise that was tailored to that person. Every time I tried that, I got a blank stare. Maybe that reaction was driven by shock; it's hard to be prepared for a question you can't even imagine based on your past experience. It can be difficult to find out how best to recognize people beyond money, even when you ask.

As James Robbins writes in his book *Nine Minutes on Monday*: "Rewarding someone usually involves giving them something tangible." Recognition "usually involves intangibles such as words of praise. . . . If a manager solely relies on [rewards] . . . she will miss out on hundreds of smaller opportunities to motivate."[55]

Doing recognition well is tough. One reason for that is we are out of practice. This is one job you shouldn't delegate. As Adrian Gostik and Chester Elton write in *24-Carrot Manager*, "To improve productivity, to enhance satisfaction, employees need recognition from you. Research shows that people accept praise and direction significantly better from their immediate supervisor than from a senior leader who they may see a couple of times a month."

The ability to impact someone's life with proper recognition is one of the great perks of leadership and often unrecognized as such. Like it or not, as a manager, you become an important person in your colleague's life, and your praise or lack of it will leave a lasting impression. Robbins writes in *Nine Minutes on Monday*, "In a study of 65 potential incentives . . . the most motivating was simply a manager who personally congratulates an employee for doing a good job."[56]

Robbins goes on to write, "The more specifically appreciation is expressed, the more powerful its effect . . ."[57] When you invest those few minutes of your time for praise, please be specific. We all know the sting of hollow praise: "Nice job!" "Way to go!" "Thanks for your support!" When you make the commitment to deliver praise, the incremental investment for specificity has a big payoff. If you can't genuinely come up with something that struck you as wonderful, skip the praise this time.

It's easy to confuse activity with achievement, so don't take the easy way out and say: "Thanks for doing X." Recognize the behaviors that are important to the organization—for working smarter, not just longer. "Thanks for missing your son Jake's baseball game to get that proposal out. We're falling behind our plan and we needed your touch on that pitch to have the best chance of closing it." He'll still be disappointed to miss the game, but the extra thirty seconds to write something specific will take away a bit of the sting.

Stories have lasting impact as recognition and appreciation. They get related over and over as examples for others to follow. For the story, set up the Situation (the problem), the Action (what specifically was done), the Impact (the specific measurable result), and Link it to values, purpose, and/or goals. The appreciation should be personal and meaningful—tell the story behind the meaning of the recognition.

> Stories have lasting impact as recognition and appreciation.

With today's calendar tools, it's easy to set annual reminders of birthdays and anniversaries. A small incremental investment of another thirty seconds turns that automated anniversary reminder into an authentic appreciation for how that colleague has made an impact and a sincere thank-you for their service.

Calendar reminders are good for building habits. Practices are stronger when they become habit. As Robbins writes in *Nine Minutes on Monday*: At the end of every week, your staff will have achieved any number of things—some big, most small. "Each one of these achievements is a potential opportunity for you" to recognize them with specific praise on that achievement. "Every day in the office, more good things happen than bad", so stop policing "and find someone exhibiting a behavior that you want to see again."[58] Most people don't know what their gifts are, but everyone has them. "By highlighting employees' personal qualities and characteristics, you place value on them as people."[59]

This is a habit that impacts many other aspects of thriving.

I'm confident that nobody gets enough recognition. I felt that as an employee, and I felt it especially as a CEO; people were either afraid to be viewed as kissing up, or they were actually kissing up—either way, genuine recognition is hard to come by for a CEO.

Praise from a trusted peer is particularly impactful. I've saved a few handwritten notes of recognition. When times are tough, I pull those out and read them for inspiration and courage. I keep a note on my wall with feedback from an intern who said: "I will take many things with me . . . most importantly knowledge about what kind of company I want to work for." I care deeply about the kind of business we created, so that unsolicited comment meant a lot to me.

Bringing It Home

Gratitude and recognition are powerful tools at home, too. My folks were Depression-era kids. They didn't grow up getting a lot of positive recognition. They didn't know a lot about how to deliver that to their kids. Generations of parents and leaders are getting better at this. Tying it to values and positive behaviors does even more at home than it does at work, because you're catching them when their suitcases of experiences are empty and waiting to be filled. This is one of those places where there might be more good parenting books about gratitude and recognition than there are business books about those subjects. The same rules apply: specific, timely, genuine, tied to desired behaviors, and avoiding the easy trap of monetary rewards. Gratitude demonstrates humility and grace. If you want your kids to keep their feet on the ground and appreciate what they have, lead by example and show appreciation for what they're doing right, early and often.

The book *The 24-Carrot Manager* is loaded with other ideas for low-cost ways to express appreciation and recognize performance. Each is more powerful when accompanied by a handwritten note that is short, specific, and authentic. Offering frequent and specific appreciation is something I would desperately encourage my younger self to do, because I certainly didn't do it enough.

See appendix 5 for a list of ideas for expressing gratitude.

TAKEAWAYS

- Gratitude accelerates thriving by delivering necessary nourishment to both the giver and the receiver. There are many ways to express gratitude beyond monetary rewards. Regular gratitude improves employee retention, employee engagement, and customer satisfaction. Valuing employees means happier customers and usually leads to higher sales and profits.

- Monetary incentives are complicated and can lead to surprising results, so they should be used carefully. Service awards and employee referral bonuses are two monetary rewards that are useful and safe. Often a heartfelt note or gift says thank-you better than money.

- As a leader, your praise, or lack thereof, has more power than many other people. Your ability to recognize and appreciate your people is a great gift for you and is nourishment for your team. Make sure your praise is genuine, specific, and timely.

- Tying appreciation to values and positive behaviors does wonders at home as well as at work.

QUESTIONS AND ACTIONS

- Think for a few minutes about praise you've received recently. Think about how you felt when someone genuinely expressed appreciation for something you did. Now, before those feelings fade, write one sincere and specific thank-you to someone.

- Think about how you felt when one of your

people handed in their resignation. Spend five minutes thinking about what happened and how you felt. Before moving on, write a short note of appreciation to one of your team members.

- Spend the next week focused on catching people doing something right. Tell them when you see it or quickly jot a short note or text explaining what you saw. How did you feel at the end of that week?

- Make a list of ways that you can express gratitude without money. Whenever you're thinking about thanking someone, pull out that list and try something new.

PART 3

1-2-1 PROCESS

ENSURING CONTINUED ALIGNMENT TOWARD MUTUAL SUCCESS

STRUGGLING WITH

SAGGING
PERFORMANCE?

➡ **Fix that TODAY with 1-2-1!** ⬅
No pills, no injections, no more worries!

Just minutes a day and you'll immediately see:

- ☑ Vigorous engagement, alignment, and performance
- ☑ Warmer working relationships among colleagues
- ☑ Crystal-clear job responsibilities and better hiring
- ☑ Regular and timely two-way feedback
- ☑ Fair and honest performance appraisals
- ☑ Open and respectful dialogue about compensation

ACT NOW!

1-2-1 PROCESS INTRODUCTION

top laughing, this is serious stuff. Okay, you can keep laughing. At least, I hope you're laughing. Look, it was a joke. 1-2-1 can't really do all that in just minutes a day.

Or maybe it can. The 1-2-1 Process is a little like the old Fram oil filter commercial. (If you're younger than fifty, you might have to Google that.) The punch line in this ad is delivered by a greasy mechanic: "You can pay me now or pay me later." In other words, if you don't take the time to do routine maintenance, something is going to break down, and that will be expensive and time-consuming.

One thing I noticed about organizations is that we often treat them worse than we treat our homes or our cars. We rarely set aside time to step off the treadmill and work on the organization itself. We mow the lawn, clean the house, paint the fence. We change the oil, vacuum the inside, and check the tire pressures. Organizationally, we don't seem to establish routine maintenance.

Looking back on my prior work experience didn't help me much. The practices I found were lacking: annual performance discussions with my manager that didn't feel right; job descriptions that didn't tell everyone what I was really responsible for doing; no good mechanism for setting goals, prioritizing them, and being accountable for my results. The grand plan was rolled out, then, forgotten as we all jumped back on the treadmill. I continued to feel around in the dark for a better way.

The first pieces of the puzzle began to come together during a visit to the Center for Positive Organizations. We sat down for an impromptu discussion with one of the founding members of the Center, Professor Kim Cameron, who told us about the Personal Management Interview (PMI) and pointed us to a 1983 paper on the subject by R. Wayne Boss titled, "Team Building and the Problem of Regression."

"PMI is a regular, private meeting between the supervisor and one of his or her immediate subordinates."[60] The paper describes how the PMI was used to impact performance following team building exercises. The data clearly show that performance improved upon implementing PMI, declined when it was halted, and improved again when it was reinstated. As I mentioned earlier, engineers love data. But I'm not sure I love data enough to have started looking for research published in 1983. Still, there it was: a simple practice that was shown to improve performance.

And the PMI fit with our gut feeling that we needed to institutionalize a way to encourage regular feedback between manager and employee. At this time, it was becoming more and more apparent that regular feedback was needed to replace the traditional annual appraisal. People couldn't wait all year to get input on performance. Annual discussions lacked the specificity of regular feedback—memories fade quickly and few of us took good enough notes along the way.

Around this time, articles began to appear about replacing the annual appraisal in favor of a timelier performance discussion—among them were pronouncements from *Harvard Business Review* and Deloitte that leading organizations around the world are scrapping the annual review and replacing it with frequent check-ins and coaching designed to promote continuous development. One researcher cited by *HBR* estimated that 70 percent of multinational companies were moving away from annual appraisal. PMI provided a framework for regular discussions that was backed by data demonstrating results.[61]

There was a surprise benefit hiding in that 1983 paper: role negotiation. The paper discusses an initial meeting between supervisor and subordinate that was held to kick off the PMI. This role negotiation meeting "dealt with specific and detailed expectations (in addition to those specified in the formal job description) that the [supervisor] and each subordinate had of one another."[62]

Two things in that sentence jumped out at me. First, the mention of the duties outlined "in the formal job description." Second, the discussion was about the expectations that manager and subordinate "had of one another."

Have you ever read a formal job description for your own job? Have you ever had one that you felt accurately described what you were responsible for? Have you ever tried to write one yourself?

I contend that most organizations have file drawers full

of formal job descriptions that rarely see the light of day. We were advised by employment attorneys that job descriptions had to be written to protect the company from litigation. We dutifully used free tools to create them for every job and filed them away. We treated them like a check-the-box exercise, and they had no impact on our organization—until that article from 1983.

The idea of role negotiation caused us to revisit the job description. One of the many complaints from employees is that managers have no idea what individuals really do. Oddly enough, once I became management, I realized that was more accurate than I'd want to admit. I also realized that employees have no idea what managers are responsible for, either. The role negotiation concept fit one of our overarching goals: getting colleagues on the same side of the table, facing problems together. Role negotiation became the genesis for our Position Alignment and resulted in a number of important surprise benefits unrelated to the PMI.

The PMI itself initially posed a marketing problem. "Personal Management Interview" was too long and didn't sound like anything I really wanted to be involved with while wearing my employee hat. That by itself wasn't too daunting because, as everyone who ever worked knows, that name would immediately be shorted to its acronym, and soon enough nobody would know what PMI stood for. But "PMI" didn't sound very appetizing either—it just didn't sound right.

We spent exactly $0 on marketing and instead relied on our engineering minds, "Call it what it is" being the familiar mantra. Well, it's a one-to-one discussion between manager and employee, so let's call it the 1-2-1. Call it what it is + use numbers if possible = every engineer's solution to a marketing problem. The PMI became the 1-2-1 Check-in and helped establish regular two-way feedback. We still had the question about the annual appraisal. At that point, almost every company we ever heard about continued to have a formal appraisal. Employment attorneys continued to advise us that we'd need something formal if we got into disputes about disciplinary actions and terminations. Appraisals dictated performance rankings, which dictated salary increases. It seemed like that was carved into the back of the tablets that Moses brought down from the mountain.

None of that fit our experience. Appraisals could not be done formulaically, no matter how much we wanted the safety of a formula. Inspired by larger companies coming to a similar conclusion, we reconsidered the goal of the appraisal.

Why do we want a learning organization? A study conducted by IBM found that 84 percent of employees in the best performing organizations received the training they needed, compared with 16 percent in the worst performing companies. Only 21 percent of new hires intend to stay at companies that don't offer training, while 62 percent will stay if training is offered.[63] A study by LinkedIn found that a majority of employees and leaders say retention is linked to the strength of a company's learning programs.[64] More than six years of research by Josh Bersin found that a learning culture improves productivity, customer satisfaction, cost structure, time to market, market share, innovation, and agility.[65]

Lifelong learning "offers each individual the ability to be, and continue to be, their best and most enlightened selves as contributors to the organization. In turn, it offers the organization . . . the ability to be, and continue to be, the best and most enlightened version of itself as an organization."[66] How do we establish such a culture? What practices support the right conditions for learning?

Learning is a cycle that we often short-circuit. We start by planning our work. Everyone does that in some way, shape, or form. Likewise, virtually everyone acts. We become conditioned to planning and acting. The treadmill goes around and around, and we run on it in the cycle of plan, act, plan, act, plan...until we are out of breath. Busyness becomes the currency of success. We don't step off the treadmill for fear that we'll be called out for not accomplishing enough. As Pink Floyd say in their song "Time," "So you run and you run to catch up with the sun," until we are not sure where we are anymore. Busy becomes much easier than thinking, though, in the end, much less satisfying.

Learning cannot take place without reflection and discovery. Reflection and discovery are acts of humility; they help us identify areas of unlearning and provide motivation in an environment that is not directly tied to a score that determines compensation like traditional appraisals. Being transparent and genuine about that helps create a sense of stability to help true exploration. As Daniel Pink points out in *Drive*, one of our intrinsic motivators is mastery. We are driven to become great at what we do. We all derive great joy from leaning into our gifts and doing great work. Mastery requires reflection, and it requires discovery.

Once again, being engineers, we decided to call it what it is: a Reflection on what happened over the last year. And since we already had a good number to use as a brand, it made us feel warm all over to call it the 1-2-1 Reflection. Individuals must do a Reflection at least annually, though they are encouraged to do them more often.

With the Reflection as the guiding star of the learning culture, the Development section was a natural extension. We wanted a process that encouraged open dialogue about each colleague's hopes and dreams, including that elephant in the room, compensation. Within each Position Alignment, we carved out time and responsibility for making yourself better. For our leaders, we added the responsibility of helping make each member of your team better. Imagine what we could do if manager and employee came together on the same side of the table to work on creating a better version of both manager and employee.

Like a jigsaw puzzle, it got easier as we assembled more pieces. The idea of the Company Alignment was brazenly borrowed from one of our larger sister companies. I loved how they captured the essence of their current and future state on one page. For years, one of the lowest ranked questions on our employee survey was essentially this: "Does senior management have a plan?" Does our team understand where we are and where we are trying to go? Can we engage people if they don't? The Company Alignment is a one-page map for where we are and where we are going.

I left the topic of goal setting for last because we are still trying to solve that problem as I write this. We experimented with a number of different processes for years before adopting Objective and Key Results (OKR). Our team has just gone into its second year with OKR, so it is a long way from being stitched into the organizational quilt. It has proven to be the best goal setting and tracking process we've ever adopted and is supported by a host of affordable tools that make it easy to institutionalize.

As the pieces of the puzzle came together, we decided to implement them all at the same time under the 1-2-1 umbrella. You, dear reader, don't have to eat this whole elephant in one bite. In the end, we didn't either, despite wrapping the whole thing under the same brand. We followed good change management practices and tackled the easier stuff first. If you think you'll have a better chance of keeping your organization aligned and thriving with a written plan for routine maintenance, read on.

CHAPTER 13

1-2-1 CHECK-INS

"When the choice is between you and me, look
for a way to explore us, the relationship itself."[67]

O ne of our leaders said the following during training at one of our annual meetings: "I know you want to avoid it, but if you have to go to your manager, at least you'll have some help managing the situation." While I'm sure I've thought something like that with my employee hat on, that statement disappointed me as a leader. I thought we had turned the corner and were working together as colleagues.

How many of your managers have you considered to be impediments instead of partners? How often was your manager your most valuable resource?

I stopped the meeting and asked those questions of our team. Isn't it difficult enough to succeed as an organization without wasting what should be the most productive partnership you have? How do we foster the conditions for making the manager-employee relationship a formidable organizational asset? For us, it began with regular one-on-one meetings.

Per that 1983 research paper on PMI, these regular meetings were held either weekly, biweekly, or monthly and they normally lasted thirty to sixty minutes. The paper says, "The major objectives . . .were to increase effective communication between the superior and the subordinate, to resolve problems, and to increase personnel accountability."[68] Part of that definition might have worked in 1983, but it didn't work for us now.

Talking about "superior" and "subordinate" is contrary to our objectives. It immediately pushes people onto separate sides of the table. This doesn't mean that the reporting relationship doesn't exist. In the end, someone must sign his or her name to contracts and be legally liable for what happens in the business. Someone must take ultimate responsibility. Someone must create a vision and make difficult day-to-day decisions. People need to be hired or let go. I don't believe that structure itself is bad. I believe that organizations get into trouble when leaders think about their jobs as perks and power rather than humility and responsibility.

> The strongest, most productive institution over a
> long period of time is one in which, all other things
> being equal, there is the largest amount of voluntary

action in support of the goals. The people do the right things at the right time to optimize total effectiveness because the goals are clear, they believe they are the right things to do and they take the necessary actions without being instructed. No institution achieves this perfectly, but the one that achieves the most of this voluntary action will be judged strong.[69]

The tricky part for leadership is how to create the right atmosphere for the maximum amount of voluntary effort in support of the organization's goals. For a manager, life is much easier if everyone does what they are supposed to do with great skill and few issues. Any manager can lead a team of low-maintenance, high-performing people. How do leaders create a place where people can optimize effectiveness because goals are clear and people do the right things?

Building relationships based on trust and respect is critical. Mutual respect grows when we honestly work to understand the other person's point of view and work together on problems. A 1-2-1 Check-in is an essential practice for keeping manager and employee on the same side of the table, looking at problems together. It maintains alignment and builds trust and respect.

> Mutual respect grows when we honestly work to understand the other person's point of view and work together on problems.

I like that the PMI definition includes "resolve problems and. . . increase personnel accountability." However, I would've liked the word "personal" instead of "personnel." And personal accountability should mean for both manager and employee as individuals and as colleagues together and not the traditional accountability of the subordinate to the superior.

This is one of the critical factors in the success of the 1-2-1 Check-in: it cannot be the traditional session where the employee is called in to the manager's office to report on what she's been doing. That would be contrary to our values and would erode trust. As we say in our one-pager on Trust:

> We believe people are inherently good—our people are skilled adults who want to do their best to deliver quality results. We trust employees to make meaningful decisions, and employees want the responsibility and freedom that comes with trust and accountability.

If I call you into my office on a regular basis to report on all the things you've been doing since our last meeting, we're not living up to our values or creating a relationship founded in trust, mutual respect, and personal accountability. Instead, this reinforces that power is in the hands of the superior. It puts the subordinate on the other side of the table, in defensive posture, focused on protection instead of an open and honest dialogue about shared goals.

At this point you might be thinking of the saying: trust but verify. The Russian proverb that was employed by Ronald Reagan during the Cold War is not a bad idea. People will violate your trust from time to time. It's happened to every one of us at some point. This is why goal setting and accountability are important. However, it shouldn't be my responsibility as your manager to chase around after you to make sure you've done your job. If we get to that point in our relationship, it's highly likely that our working relationship is coming to an end.

A key goal of the 1-2-1 Check-in is to put the responsibility where it belongs: with the colleague. You are a trusted and skilled adult. You don't want to be micro-managed. You want to make meaningful decisions and you want to be able to guide your own actions. Heck, you might have a little human being at home that you're responsible for yourself. You should start by being the boss of you. In our world, the onus of scheduling and managing the 1-2-1 Check-in is on the employee and not the manager.

> A key goal of the 1-2-1 Check-in is to put the responsibility where it belongs: with the colleague.

This is important for a few reasons. First, it demonstrates that the colleague recognizes the value of the partnership with her manager. Traditionally, employees do everything they can to avoid the manager. They want to avoid accountability, and the manager's main job is to hold them accountable. That's not the way a positive, thriving organization works. That's not what drives the maximum voluntary effort toward the organization's goals. If my team views me as an obstacle to be avoided, then should I be in a position of leadership at all? I should be the single most valuable resource you have. I should help you prioritize your responsibilities, think through your problems, remove roadblocks, help you recognize your gifts, help you reach your goals and become a better version of yourself. Can your peers do all that for you like I can?

Second, it turns a reporting session into a problem-solving session. The colleague should set the agenda for the meeting—after all, it's his meeting. "We have thirty to sixty minutes together: What do you want to accomplish? What's the most important thing we should discuss? How can I help?"

If my colleague doesn't set the meeting and send me an agenda, then we need to talk about the process to make sure he understands how this is supposed to work and reinforce that this is his responsibility and not the traditional "What have you been doing?" session. Many people were raised on that diet, and old habits die hard. Some unlearning may be needed. I should make sure his failure to take initiative isn't because he's carrying around a lot of useless baggage from past work experiences.

If I've done what I can to ensure that he understands the process, but he still avoids me, we have a different issue. Maybe it really isn't you, it's me. Do I have the same issue with other members of my team? Have other managers had the same issue with him? We need to sit down and talk through our relationship openly. We cannot go very far without a certain level of mutual respect and trust. We may need help from HR to work us through the issue.

Sounds painful? Would you rather just wait and die the death of a thousand cuts? Going home frustrated because he's not meeting your expectations; complaining to others; talking to HR about disciplinary actions and what you can do to terminate him; going back to the market to interview many more candidates, then onboard and train the new person. Or maybe if you wait long enough, he'll take the decision out of your hands and leave on his own. If all that happens, can you look yourself in the eye and honestly say that you did everything you reasonably could to help him succeed?

Let's go back to our 1983 research paper again, which says:

> . . . as long as a supportive relationship exists, subordinates are free to deal with and resolve the problems that will inevitably arise with their peers without fear of retaliation by the leader. Furthermore, when the leader expects subordinates to deal constructively with conflicts that exist between peers, norms are quickly established that foster healthy, viable teams. Since conflict cannot be prevented, such expectations force team members to deal with inevitable conflict constructively and use it for the betterment of the group.[70]

As a manager, have you ever been called in to referee a dispute between two colleagues? Did it feel like you were dealing with trusted and responsible adults? Do you think one of those adults ironically finds himself refereeing disputes between his children at home? How many times do people complain to you about someone else instead of taking up that issue directly and respectfully with the other person? Imagine how much better the workplace would be if people would constructively manage conflicts on their own.

The 1-2-1 Check-in establishes the bedrock on which the team is built. Solid relationships with the manager spawn better relationships amongst colleagues. The Check-in also offers the proper venue for coaching on conflict resolution in a setting that says, "We're working this issue together in a proactive way so that I'm not surprising you with a situation down the road." And we're addressing potential issues together, whether they are personnel related or not, and trying to head off any issues early on and not in crisis. In my experience, going too long between Check-ins increases the probability that something will break without warning and perhaps catastrophically.

The 1-2-1 Check-in establishes the bedrock on which the team is built.

If you're worried about finding time to meet with each of your people at least monthly for thirty to sixty minutes, remember that old Fram oil filter commercial: you can pay me now or pay me later. Invest in the relationship and it will pay dividends. You'll hear about problems when they are smaller. I'd rather fight a little baby dragon than go up against Godzilla, especially when I get to do that with you and when we are not in crisis. Avoid the mutual stress of those situations and create the right environment to talk about those things before they become more intractable.

Each of us is routinely approached by others for help. This means we are almost constantly making decisions about resources and priorities. Regular discussions can help us assess all of those new commitments that other people want to put on your plate. What do you think you should do about those? How should we prioritize this new request? Anything that will soak up a lot of your time should be a conversation, especially if it will impact your ability to deliver on the commitments we've already established. As your manager, I should be helping to preserve your relationship by taking responsibility for saying no to a new request and flying cover for you.

Every Position Alignment carves out time for personal and professional development. In a learning environment, we're trying to encourage people to identify and develop their gifts. Marcus Buckingham and Curt Coffman's *First, Break all the Rules* is one of the core books in our leadership training. It encourages the positive practice of focusing on what makes people uniquely wonderful rather than on their faults. The engineer in me responds to the clear logic: you are probably happy when you are doing something that you are great at, so if we can figure out what that is and apply it to help the organization, you'll be better off and so will the organization.

The challenge is that very few people know what their gifts are. I've interviewed a lot of people and I've asked them to tell me what they're great at. Very few people can clearly articulate why God put them on this earth. Most people haven't been encouraged to figure it out. Instead, many have been told much about the things they are not good at and need to improve. Mastery is a great intrinsic motivator, but how can you be a master at anything if you don't know what your gifts are? How can you develop a healthy sense of self without the belief that you do some things really well?

Developing your people isn't just a way to create a motivated and productive workplace. It's an opportunity for you to change a life. When you are gone, how will you be remembered? Of all the leaders you've had yourself, how many of them do you remember fondly? Why? Could it be that they helped you recognize your gifts and develop them? What did that do to your life—not just your career, but your life?

Despite carving time out for development, most people don't take time to work on it. We get stuck on the treadmill of activity. We don't want to take time to learn new things. Our leaders should use Check-in time to make sure that doesn't happen and to hold you accountable for the goals you've set to make yourself better. We didn't do this very well in our business—but I'm confident it happened more than it would have if we did not set aside that time in the Position Alignment and encouraged all of our team to hold each other accountable during Check-ins.

The most important benefit of the Check-in is that people need regular and specific feedback. Annual appraisals are dying, in part, because we struggle to come up with specific examples that should have been delivered in the moment. Issues can fester, grow, and become intractable if left untreated.

We struggle to come up with specific examples that should have been delivered in the moment. Issues can fester, grow, and become intractable if left untreated.

Regular feedback goes both ways. Managers are made and not born. There's not some special factory that produces leaders. They come in all shapes and sizes. Leadership is a lifelong learning experience. Mastery should motivate us as leaders to constantly seek out feedback that helps us improve. Good leaders will admit that they don't have it figured out and are not sure about what they're doing much of the time. How can we improve if we don't get regular feedback from the people who are best equipped to give it to us? Unfortunately, it's difficult to get good honest and specific feedback from our people. Tradition and organizational baggage present barriers. Retribution is feared. The relationship has to be on solid footing to have any chance of getting good feedback from our people. The Check-in helps establish that feedback over time and provides the venue for it to be given.

If we are handling the Check-in like any important meeting, there's an agenda and notes. We should each be prepared for the meeting and have an influence on the agenda. If I go into any meeting without my own objectives, I get what I deserve. If I don't take notes and assign clear action items, then we've wasted the organization's time and money. It's another sign of mutual respect that we treat the Check-in like any other important meeting. We should be sure to review our action items from our last meeting and treat those as we would any other responsibility that we're accountable for. We're professionals, and we go about our business with purpose.

The notes from these Check-ins become a regular script for the story of our year. When it's time for Reflection, I can look back through my Check-in notes and get a clear picture of what happened. I inevitably remember an accomplishment that I'd forgotten about. I can see a failure coming when I look back at how it unfolded, and that helps me reflect and learn.

These notes are also essential for Talent Review time. They provide specific examples of performance that give me the objective evidence I need to make a case for a specific increase. They help me assess feedback from other teams. They give me context for performance and examples of how that person contributed in ways beyond just achieving goals. They identify specific talents and potential that the organization needs to develop further.

Maybe your organization already does this, maybe it doesn't. This is clearly something that you can do, no matter where you are in an organization. All the benefits and reasons above are there for the taking. You just have to commit to the time investment and genuinely treat this as an important meeting between colleagues. Be the leader your people dream about, and maybe they will be more likely to become the colleague you dream about.

Bringing It Home

If you wonder whether this can work for your family, go back and read that quote from the research paper about handling conflicts and problems independently. I know a lot of families that conduct regular one-on-one check ins with their kids informally. This might be a father-daughter date night or time driving one of the kids to soccer practice. If you've had that time as a parent, you probably feel like it was a wonderful gift. [Maybe not so much during the teen years.] Can you manage a monthly one-on-one with each kid for thirty or sixty minutes? If you're doing this already, does this section help put the effort into a different light? If you start doing this, do you see performance improve over time? Maybe there's not an agenda, but does that regular dialogue break down some of the barriers and allow information to flow more freely? Does that help send a more independent problem solver off to college or the working world?

As I finish this section, I look back with a bit of wonder that all this organizational booty was found in an old chest from 1983 that was hidden in the attic until a chance encounter pointed us in the right direction.

Please see appendix 1 for a short checklist to help enable your own Check-ins.

TAKEAWAYS

- A regular 1-2-1 Check-in helps turn the traditionally antagonistic manager-employee relationship into a partnership focused on excellence. Done well, the Check-in can turn your manager from avoided impediment into your most valuable resource.

- The manager-employee relationship is one of the most important relationships you will have. It requires effort to build and maintain—as does any good relationship. When it's not working, it's painful for both parties. An investment in the Check-in will pay off many times over.

- This is not the traditional check-in where the manager expects the employee to report on his activities. This is a two-way discussion among partners focused on success: for the organization and for the individual employee.

- The onus is on the employee to schedule the

Check-in. Both parties are responsible for being prepared, setting an agenda, taking action items, building a trusting relationship, and providing each other with on-going feedback that helps build a strong partnership.

- Key activities include adjusting priorities as needed, removing roadblocks to success, giving specific and timely feedback, recognizing and celebrating success, identifying strengths, and helping each other create better versions of ourselves.

- Notes from your regular Check-ins provide valuable and specific information for performance assessments, compensation reviews, gratitude, and real-time feedback.

- The Check-in is scientifically proven to improve performance and reduce stress.

QUESTIONS AND ACTIONS

- How do you get timely feedback today? Think about something you are very good at. How did regular feedback help you master that activity?

- Does your manager have a clear understanding of what you do and the value you bring? Are you frustrated by changing priorities? Would you like to have a broader understanding of what's going on in the business? How can you actively change the present situation? Would your job satisfaction improve if your manager was your most valuable resource?

- What would happen if you treated each of your employees with the same respect as you do your own manager or your board of directors? Take six months and invest in Check-ins with a mutual agenda focused on what your people need. Stop after six months. Is there a difference?

- How do you do performance reviews for yourself and others? Do you keep notes throughout the year about key accomplishments, challenges, and development opportunities?

- How do you do Check-ins with your significant other or your kids? Can you make this a routine practice without making it awkward? After you've tried it for six months, reflect back on the practice and what you learned. Was it worth the effort?

CHAPTER 14

POSITION ALIGNMENT

What would you say you do here?

Engagement, better hiring, job crafting, resource allocation, retention, job satisfaction, respect, communication, understanding . . . all from watching a YouTube clip from an old movie.

Have you seen the 1999 movie *Office Space*? If not, search YouTube for "The Two Bobs scene." Go ahead, I'll wait. . . .Okay, you're back, and you're laughing, so that's good. When we introduced the concept of the Position Alignment to our colleagues, we started with that video. Everyone was laughing. As Bob number one looks at poor Tom and says, "What would you say . . . you do here?", you are laughing, but a little piece of you might be saying to yourself, "I'm glad I'm not in Tom's seat."

Then we put them in that seat. Not, of course, with the threat that we were going to put people out of a job. Not even with the faintest thought that we were putting anyone out of a job. We approached it with the genuine curiosity about whether each individual could clearly describe what they did for the team in terms others could understand. It's important to have a good relationship and a foundation of trust before going down this road. If your organization is like the one in *Office Space*, you might want to work on Foundational Practices before you tackle Position Alignment.

We started this exercise on a small group of lab rats (otherwise known as our leadership team) so we could see what would happen in a controlled setting. We showed the movie clip. Everyone laughed. We handed everyone a sheet of paper and asked them to write it out on one page of paper, "what are the three to five buckets of responsibility you have to the team, and what are the key components of those key responsibilities." "Seriously?" they said. "Yup," we said. "Ooo-kay, but this won't take long."

Pencils went to paper, and then they froze. Heads were scratched. More paper was handed out, and eventually pencil sharpeners had to be found and passed around. It's a simple question: "What do you do here?" I should know the answer, and I should be able to write that down on one page of paper in terms you can understand. If you want leadership to capture our company's higher purpose, values, vision, and goals on one sheet of paper, surely you can explain what you do in that amount of space.

Eventually, with some examples and quite a few drafts, everyone got there. People with the same job title could at least get together and compare notes. We found that even with the same title, there were variations in responsibilities. We are still relatively small and think of ourselves as being lean and entrepreneurial, which means that people pick up tasks that might be outside of their initial purview because there was nobody else to do that task as we grew. Over time, as we adopted more of these practices, people picked up tasks outside of their "job" that played to their talents.

Organizationally, though, that wasn't captured anywhere. Our canned job descriptions sat unused in electronic files and offered only the vaguest idea of what that role was supposed to be doing for the team. The Position Alignment became the first real and accurate description of each individual's responsibilities to the team. What started out as a fun challenge about individual accountability to the team became so much more than that.

The first surprise was personal. I had never thought about communicating what I did for the organization. Like everyone in the company, I thought that was clear. I'm obviously busy all the time and delivering value—surely people can see that and know what I do. If nothing else, I knew what I did and what I was responsible for. Or so I thought. The problem is, I never tried to write it down.

There's something magical about writing something down. Many times I thought I had something completely figured out in my head, but when I sat down to write it out so others could understand it, at some point I almost inevitably stopped in my tracks and said: "Well, *that* doesn't work." We think we've got it. We think others got it. Inevitably though, when we sit down and write it out, we don't got it. Either there's a flaw in our plan, or we're on two different pages.

After a few drafts, I was able to explain my role as CEO. I had four main responsibilities to the organization: I was part-time General Counsel, managing legal issues, I was part-time Chief Financial Officer, part-time Chief People Officer, and part-time CEO. Each of those roles had a number of bullet points describing what that meant. My fifth role, as with every other manager, was to develop myself and my team. I was surprised how much more difficult the exercise was, and I was surprised at the clarity it provided me in my role.

There's something magical about writing something down.

I was also surprised at the reaction by others. Most people didn't know what I really did and why it could be valuable to the organization. Yes, of course, they understood in broad terms that the company needs a CEO, the leader, the big cheese, the place where the buck stops. That's about it, though. Ask someone what I really did for a living, and there was a lot of hemming and hawing.

Because I operated in a number of roles, the Position Alignment allowed me to be more specific in my interactions with people. Am I asking this from you as the CEO or as the CFO? That may sound trivial, but people react differently to a question from the CEO than they would from the General Counsel. This is even more valuable now that I am the ex-CEO.

The next surprise was when we asked people to tell us how much time they spent on each one of those buckets of responsibility. Then we asked them to tell us how much time they *wanted* to spend on each of those buckets of responsibility. We didn't do this because we knew what was coming. We just did it out of curiosity for how much of their job was spent on each role. Asking the first question was helpful for resource planning. Asking the second question was where the magic happened.

How do you identify a person's talents? If we agree that we want to focus on strengths, and most people can't articulate what those are, how do we find the darned things?

People generally spend time on what they love to do and they generally are very good at what they love to do. We started with a simple question about responsibility and resource allocation. We wanted to know that everyone knew where we were deploying our most important resources. What we got was that and more. Regular discussions about the *want to* spend time could begin to tease out talent in a systematic way. It could allow us to narrow in on

> People generally spend time on what they love to do and they generally are very good at what they love to do.

why you love that part of the job, begin to turn the why into a defined talent, and begin to have real conversations about getting you to do more of what you want to do.

The "don't want to spend time" was interesting too. What's driving you crazy about your responsibilities today? Not in a general "this job sucks" way around the water cooler or in the local tavern, but a respectful, safe discussion aimed at deploying resources more efficiently. Sometimes there is someone on the same team or in the same group that might love that bucket of responsibility and hates the one you love. Imagine if that happens and you can make two people happier and more productive at the same time.

Or maybe it's a question of not having the tools or information needed to do the job. Or because of a relationship problem with a key colleague. Here's another way to open that dialogue and help do something about it in a safe environment. Not as a complaint, not shirking responsibilities, not a whiney "I don't wanna," but a measured discussion about resource allocation, weaknesses, and how they can be overcome in a team setting. This is another way you can become a valued resource for your colleague instead of an impediment.

People thought I loved the General Counsel role. They saw the attention I gave to it and figured that I loved it. In fact, I hated it. I took on that role because I couldn't find anyone else that would do it and I knew that mistakes in that role could be very expensive. The "don't wanna" view helped me go from a martyr/victim to seeking help and restructuring my responsibilities. I still hung onto the role, but I got a lot more help with prompting from my management. This came from me pointing out that I'd like to do more CFO and CEO work and less work as the untrained in-house lawyer.

Job crafting is an appealing idea to many people. If we can really craft individual responsibilities around skills, we can all be happier and more productive, making better use of our biggest assets. How to do that has always been a big question. The Position Alignment provided us with a mechanism to pursue it. The measure of how much time spent in each role doesn't have to be very precise. It can be a ballpark estimate. The point is to seek out the mismatches between *want* and *don't want* and have grounded discussions about them. It's not foolproof, but at least there is some basis for the discussion.

Let's go back to 1983 again for a moment. Go get that Members Only jacket out of the closet and put on the soundtrack to *Grosse Pointe Blank*. Remember the "role negotiation" part of the Personal Management Interview. The idea behind role negotiation is that you sit down with your manager and talk about what you do here. Um, exqueeze me? Baking powder? Negotiation?! We negotiated a salary and a starting date, and I showed up when I was supposed to and went to work. What's this negotiation stuff?

When you were hired, how clear were your responsibilities? Sure, there was a job description, and if you were careful, you might have even asked some more questions about how much time was spent on this or that. When you actually started to do the job, did you really know what you were in for? Did you know that 75 percent of your HR job was going to be recruiting? Did you know that VP of Sales and Marketing really meant VP of Sales? How clearly do we really understand what our responsibilities are when we show up?

When you were hired, how clear were your responsibilities?

If we don't know, then it's hard to negotiate. With *want / don't want* percentages and a Position Alignment, we really could do a role negotiation. Do I know which parts of your job you love to do and want to do more of? Is there any way we can intentionally craft how you spend your time? If we have that discussion and genuinely look for ways to do that, is it easier for you to accept some responsibilities you really don't like? As we grow and I know what people want to do more of, can I create a role that is built for what my team doesn't want to do? With the Position Alignment in hand, we finally understood the concept of role negotiation.

The next big surprise benefit of the Position Alignment was its impact on the hiring process. Before, a manager would approach her manager to ask for more resources or a new position, and the discussion was virtually entirely about budget: Can we afford it? Did we budget for it? Some vague discussion about justifying the need ensued. In the end, it often depended on how good the manager was at selling the idea or how trustworthy that manager was based on past resource decisions. The Position Alignment helped us have a more grounded discussion about the responsibilities of that role and whether they could be filled with other resources we had. If it was a new role, could that manager clearly define a full-time job on one sheet of paper? Did it make the process foolproof? No. It did make it a more enriching dialogue than it was before.

And it was very much appreciated by applicants. The Position Alignment became the clearest explanation of the job we ever put in front of an applicant. It was an accurate depiction of what you would be responsible for, what roles you had to play, and how much of your time would be in each role. It made for more enriching interviews about the responsibilities and whether talent fit those roles. We heard on multiple occasions that applicants appreciated the clarity and respected the time we spent defining the job. They didn't encounter the bait and switch of talking about the fun stuff and leaving out the other 75 percent. This helped improve satisfaction and retention.

Position Alignments, like User Manuals, were freely shared among the team. As with User Manuals, they helped us all have a better understanding of what other people did for the organization. Eventually, we had occasions when the team would halt the hiring process and divvy up the responsibilities amongst themselves rather than hire a new person. That's a team role negotiation and shows ownership thinking.

You could do this no matter where you are in an organization. You might not want to talk about it as a replacement for your job description. You can certainly do this for yourself. How much time are you actually spending versus "want to spend" in each role? What does that say about your interests and talents? Could you sit down with your manager and talk about your job responsibilities and use it as a guide for your development and career? Would it make it easier to have a richer discussion?

You could certainly show your people the "Two Bobs" clip and challenge them to describe what they do here. Again, you might want to make sure you have a safe relationship established. Did anything surprise you? Did you realize your people were handling things you didn't know they were doing? What happened when you asked open-ended questions about how much time they actually spend versus wanted to spend?

Bringing It Home

What does a role negotiation look like at home? I'll fill the dishwasher all day, but I hate to unload it. I'll cook, but I don't want to clean up, too. I'm hell on wheels with the checkbook, but please don't put me in charge of the 401(k). Is there a lesson there about work, autonomy, and not being a victim? Does that clarity of roles eliminate hidden frustrations and repair relationships?

You know that you have instilled change when the new way becomes part of the vernacular. Position Alignment became the way we talked about our responsibilities and those of our colleagues. It became a requirement of the hiring process. It also made it easier for us to reflect back on our accomplishments and failures, because we had a clear set of responsibilities in front of us when we sat down to give ourselves a rating.

I've included a couple of examples in appendix 2, including mine.

TAKEAWAYS

- A Position Alignment is a one-page description of your responsibilities to the organization in terms that others can understand. It organizes your duties into 3–5 "buckets" of responsibilities with bullet points of the major sub-parts. It's the most accurate and helpful job description you've ever had.

- Many people pick up duties that are never described anywhere. The organization doesn't know about these, and even the manager is often unaware. The employee often doesn't get recognized for these duties. A good Position Alignment raises awareness of roles and responsibilities.

- Employees often don't know what management really does. A good job description clarifies roles and responsibilities for everyone. It makes it easier to provide context for the requests we make of each other. It helps people better understand the value of the collective group of resources.

- The Position Alignment is a great help to the hiring process. It helps the team understand whether a new position is needed. It helps recruits understand the real responsibilities of the job, which makes the organization stand out positively and helps reduce turnover.

- Describing how much time you spend in each role versus how much time you want to spend in each role is a surprisingly effective tool for identifying talents and job crafting.

- Position Alignments can help improve the efficient use of your most valuable resource: people.

QUESTIONS AND ACTIONS

- Do you have a copy of your current job description? Does it accurately reflect what you are responsible for? If not, how could that negatively impact your performance and your standing within the organization?

- Do you know what your manager is responsible for? Would your relationship with your manager change if you had a clear understanding of her responsibilities?

- When you accepted your current job, did you find that the responsibilities you actually spent time on matched what you thought you'd spend your time on?

- What does your Position Alignment look like at work and at home? What can you learn from the "want to" versus the "don't wanna" assessment of time spent in each area of responsibility?

CHAPTER 15

COMPANY ALIGNMENT

Because leaders should be able to tell
people where we're going on one page.

N o matter how small or how big the organization is, I think most employees wonder whether there is a plan for the future. Can management explain to me what our business is about and where we're going in the short-term and longer-term? Can they do that on one page and in terms I can understand? If they can't, many people will assume that there really is no plan. This becomes another brick in the wall (excuse the *Pink Floyd* reference again): we already don't really know what senior management does on a daily basis, we do know that they are paid a lot more than we are, and now we really don't see one of the most important things they are responsible for: a clear plan.

With my senior management hat on, I can be frustrated. When I saw the relatively low marks we got on that question in our employee survey, I confess that my first emotion was outrage. It seemed like we spent all kinds of time in small and large groups talking about who we are and where we're going. How could people think we didn't have a plan? What did they think we were spending our time on?

Then I took one of my little yellow pills and a few deep breaths and I realized that this problem, like every problem, eventually stops with me. Getting frustrated doesn't help. We should be able to present a summary of who we are and what we're trying to do on one page. And again, we got a good example of how to do this from a larger company in our investors' portfolio, and we adapted it to our needs.

The page starts from the things that don't change in our business and moves to the things that do. It begins with our higher purpose. Remember that? No, not "cathodic protection on buried metal structures." I know that one was memorable, but I'm surprised it stuck in your head. No, I'm talking about protecting people and the environment by helping our energy infrastructure run safely. From Purpose, we move to values in the shorter bullet-point format. These two things form the bedrock of who we are and they guide everything we do.

The next third of a page is a summary of our five-year vision. What are the pillars of change, the focus areas for what problems we don't want to have in the future? Similar to the values, we can't try to tell the whole story here; we're just trying to trigger the collective organizational memory and remind everyone about what we set out to do. This is the hopeful outlook about how great the next version of our company will be.

The last third is what we're trying to accomplish this year.

If you're using Objectives and Key Results (OKR), this one is easy, because you've already planned at this level. What are the key accomplishments we're shooting for this year to support our longer-term vision? If OKR, this is likely to be the Objective statement and not include all of the Key Results in order to keep this to one page.

At the bottom of the page is a prompt for everyone: What are you personally doing to align with this plan? In other words, if you don't see the connection between your responsibilities and something on this page, make that the focus of your next Check-in. As a group, we can't get very far if everyone doesn't see how they fit into the bigger picture. Don't be a victim and complain that you don't know your place in the plan—if you can't find it yourself with this aid, then get some help.

> We can't get very far if everyone doesn't see how they fit into the bigger picture.

That's it. So easy that there's no good excuse not to do it. Only the annual goals need to be updated between first draft and the next five-year vision. The first third is rarely going to change. This becomes the cover sheet in each person's playbook, from high level down to you, the individual.

If you're not able to direct policy across your entire organization, you can still do this for your team. It might be a little harder if your company doesn't have a purpose or values, unless you've already created those for your group. If there's no vision, you could use the vision that you and your team created for how things can be better in five years. Certainly you will have objectives that have been handed down to you in some form or another. This is an opportunity to connect all the dots for your team, even if your overall leadership hasn't done that for the whole. You can ask the same question of each member of your team: do you understand how you fit into these goals and what we expect of you? I don't think the size of the group matters. I think people are looking for leadership to involve them in a clear plan toward achieving worthwhile objectives.

Bringing It Home

I confess that I haven't tried to create a company alignment for my family. I live with three women, so there is already plenty of eye rolling. I can see how it could work for even a small family if there is a set of values and a shared vision for the future. Maybe it's not printed up and distributed to everyone. Maybe it's handwritten and hanging on the refrigerator. Maybe it's like many lessons I never thought our kids were listening to until later in life, when I realized that they really were soaking that in and acting on it.

In the end, as leaders, one of our most important duties is to align everyone so we're all pulling in the same direction with a clear understanding of where we're going.

TAKEAWAYS

- A Company Alignment is a one-page road map for your organization. It starts with a summary of your higher purpose and your values—the enduring foundation of your organization. It provides a summary of your team's longer-term vision to keep everyone pulling in the same direction. It concludes with a summary of this year's key goals toward that longer-term vision.

- Without a good roadmap, people can get lost easily. The organization doesn't have Google Maps or Siri, so leaders need to provide the team with a short and clear map of where we're all headed together. Without that, it's hard to complain when the team isn't pulling in the same direction.

QUESTIONS AND ACTIONS

- Write a one-page Company Alignment for "your town," starting with your purpose, values, current goals, and a summary of where you want to be in five years.

- Can you do the same for your family?

CHAPTER 16

GOAL SETTING

*Clear individual accountability is the linchpin
to trust, freedom, and organizational bliss.*

O rganizations exist to achieve something. Since organizations are made up of individuals, at some point, individuals need goals of their own. The whole point of organizations is that we are better as a group than we are as individuals. As Simon Sinek said, "The human animal is a social animal, and our very survival depends on our ability to form communities . . . we are not good by ourselves. If I send you out to find a saber-toothed tiger by yourself, odds are tiger 1, you zero. . . . But if you go as a group, we're pretty damned amazing."[71]

It's likely that you never sent anyone out looking for a tiger, but we have all had some pretty difficult responsibilities and goals. We certainly achieve goals better as a group, and the nature of today's work environment is that problems are increasingly more complex and require more of us to come together to resolve them. However, we are an organization of individuals, so at some level there have to be personal accountability, goals, and metrics. Not just for performance evaluations, talent reviews, and compensation. We need these individual goals for ourselves, for our own development, growth, and satisfaction.

For us to hone our own talents and develop mastery in anything, we must have challenging goals and a way to measure our own performance.

This may be why goal setting is so difficult for most organizations. Most goals depend on help from the organization in some form. Organizations have challenges setting high-level goals and driving them down to each individual. Individuals need good goals to be motivated. Many individuals do not have a healthy sense of self and therefore have some significant fear of failure. Most organizations (and managers) do not create an environment where failure and performance are handled in a healthy way. Many organizations still go through an annual performance review that is unfair, irrational, and one-sided. I think this all leads to something I've seen throughout my career that is disappointing but not surprising.

I've found that most people want transparent accountability for everyone but themselves. I've never heard a single person say that they want to be micromanaged. Everyone wants to be a trusted adult left to do their work their way.

The challenge with goal setting is that most people want goals and transparent metrics for everyone else but themselves. I've heard people complaining about others: how they don't work as hard, don't do as much, don't deliver. But that same person, when pressed for transparency about their own performance, will often get offended that they are being called to task. The same scale bias problem on performance appraisals happens whether it is a self-appraisal or one done by management. There are many factors here that combine to make individual goal setting a challenge.

> The challenge with goal setting is that most people want goals and transparent metrics for everyone else but themselves.

Since the organization exists to achieve goals and individuals need to understand the part they play in achieving those goals, leaders need to work with the team to figure out what the overall goals are and help translate those into individual goals. That is no small task, even for a small group. If you haven't tried to do that and you question that statement, walk into the arena and try it. As the organization gets bigger, the challenge grows exponentially. This is truly one of the most difficult tasks of leadership. As with vision and values, you have to craft the organization's goals in simple enough terms that you can explain them to everyone in minutes. Yet you also have to be able to drill down to minute detail in order to connect them to everyone. Does that sound easy?

We encountered many twists along our journey to incorporate better goal setting into our 1-2-1 process. It started by confronting the challenges I've outlined above with our team.

Again, let's not sit across from each other and negotiate—let's sit on the same side of the table and look at this problem to-

Let's not sit across from each other and negotiate—let's sit on the same side of the table and look at this problem together.

gether. We all want to be trusted adults seeking individual and organization success. We want a healthy culture based on mutual respect, trust, transparency, and fairness; all heads nodding up and down. We want you to set clear goals and metrics for measuring your achievements; many heads turning side to side.

Software Development was the most vocal. "We're different," they said. "We're all working together to create code. What do you want us to do, measure how much code we write? What if some things are easy to code, and some things aren't? What if someone writes a lot of code but it's not good code? You don't need to measure us, anyway. We have clear requirements for our products and deadlines for delivery, as a group. If you start measuring how all of us code as individuals, I don't think you can do it fairly and you'll screw up the dynamics of the team and ruin everything. We have weekly meetings to talk about where everyone is in their responsibilities, and we pitch in to help anyone that's falling behind. Why don't you go measure Accounting and assign them a bunch of goals and metrics—God knows what those bean counters do, anyway."

Okay, maybe not quite that cynical. Or, maybe it was even more cynical than that. This response is happening in a culture we tried to establish for more than a decade as one built on trust and transparency. At least they were arguing with us about how to do this. I can imagine in many organizations, there would be silence, and an attitude of "take your best shot; you're going to do whatever you want anyway, so let's just get this over with."

(At this point I'd like to remind you that the title of this book is _Practically_ Positive, not _Perpetually_ Positive. I am trying to be honest about what we face in the real world. I am sure there are many organizations out there that would experience a much more difficult time chasing good goal setting than we did. Organizations are messy because people are messy. Our strengths are also our weaknesses. Our individuality and personal views are across the map. They make us stronger as a group but also make it more difficult to agree on anything.)

> Our individuality and personal views are across the map. They make us stronger as a group but also make it more difficult to agree on anything.

We talked, we cajoled, we listened, we explained our reasoning, we countered objections. We used carrots and not sticks. We looked for ways to engage the head and the heart. We didn't threaten anyone. We continued to focus on achieving excellence and growth as an organization and as individuals. We asked everyone to set individual, clear goals and metrics for the coming year within the background of our five-year vision and our overall annual company goals. We asked that they focus on meaningful goals and not list every small task they had to achieve in their daily responsibilities. We started this in Word, then moved to Excel, specifically because we thought it would be easier to track goals and progress in Excel. Challenges achieving these goals could be discussed in Check-ins.

It was a step in the right direction, but a small step. If colleagues set goals at all, they were often nebulous. We tried teaching every good goal setting process we could find. We used SMART, as so many before us had done. There are many variations on SMART; ours was Specific, Measurable, Achievable, Relevant, and Time-Bound. Achievable seemed to be the focus of most people. Time-bound was pretty easy too. Even Relevant could be worked out if we had a good mutual discussion in our Check-ins. Specific and Measurable were (and still are) the biggest challenge.

Excel was also an issue. It invited people to drive down into "to-do list" levels of detail. Every objective could be broken down into minute tasks. This is natural and necessary. One of my people was a reliable achiever because he thought through every step he needed to achieve to hit the bigger objective. The problem was that it became very difficult to have discussions about goals in the right level of detail. As a manager of five or ten people, I cannot discuss every step in the process. As a trusted adult, you shouldn't want to discuss every step. You should be able to distill this to the headlines, which is hard to do, even for senior leadership.

Management of change was another difficult issue. We might agree on a set of annual goals (or even monthly or quarterly goals). We might even agree on priority, resources, and metrics. No plan survives for very long in the real world. Things change, stuff happens, and colleagues ask you for help. How do you manage new goals while keeping track of the old ones? And in what level of detail? The Check-in, done well, helped sort out priorities, resources, and timing. Even if this was managed well, we continued to struggle to find the right level of detail for goal setting.

Toward the end of my time as CEO, my team began setting higher-level goals on a quarterly cadence. We focused on things we had to get done beyond the tactical, daily job activities. In order to hit our annual goals toward our five-year vision, what did each of us need to sign up for, how would we know what "done well" means—what's the priority, what resources are needed? It was up to the colleague to draft these and share them before a Check-in focused on this need. As manager, I would add anything critical that was missing and help prioritize goals, then we would meet to discuss and agree on the plan. We wanted a limit of five key goals per quarter, though inevitably they ended up at seven or eight. It became clear that we couldn't do much more than that and our daily jobs in a quarter if the goals were written at the right level. In each subsequent 1-2-1, we wouldn't talk about the status of each one—not in a traditional "What have you done this week?" Instead, it was focused on resolving roadblocks, resources, timing, and adjusting priorities to accommodate anything new that showed up when the bullets started to fly.

Supposedly, my team and I were the best and brightest in the organization. Yet we struggled with this exercise. It wasn't resistance or mistrust; I honestly felt that my team left that baggage behind and wasn't worried about gaming the system or repercussions from failure to meet difficult objectives. The main challenge was creating specific goals at the right level, deciding the five or six most important things we should be working on, and ensuring that everyone on our team was aware of the goals of the others so we could see how it fit together and make good decisions about priorities when peers had to work together to achieve organizational goals. We also needed to manage change and drive those goals down throughout all teams to each individual. We needed to come up with a clear understanding of what "done" means and a quantitative metric to measure that. What we were doing was working better than anything we'd tried so far, but it was still very difficult. Other issues we faced were using Word, OneNote, or Teams to track these goals, communicating and creating visibility, and still being unsure about whether we were doing this the right way.

My successor drove the next major iteration in our goal-setting process. He heard about Objectives and Key Results (OKR) and started reading up on it. As I was transitioning out, he adopted OKR across the organization and got training for the team. As I read up on it, I saw that it was a more formal version of what we had been doing in our last iteration. OKR is "a methodology that helps to ensure that the company focuses efforts on the same important issues throughout the organization."[72] An Objective is a description of what is to be achieved and is significant, concrete, action-oriented, and in-spirational. A Key Result is a specific, time-bound, aggressive, yet realistic benchmark for monitoring whether the objective was achieved. This is what we were trying to practice without knowing about OKR.

It was backed by a wealth of experience by many success-ful organizations. It was adopted by Andy Grove, the former longtime leader at Intel, when he observed that "There are so many people working so hard and achieving so little."[73] Many books have been written about it, and there was a wealth of training resources, including one leading expert in our own backyard. As our CEO said when he first told me about OKR, "This really fits with our culture."

"Transparency is the default setting for our daily lives. It's the express lane to operational excellence. Yet at most companies, goals remain secrets" (as do the responsibilities of each person to the organization). "Research shows public goals are much more likely to be attained. . . . When people write down 'This is what I'm working on,' it's easier to see where the best ideas are coming from. Soon it's apparent that the individuals moving up are the ones doing what the company most values."[74] Suspicion, sandbagging, politics—they lose their power. Transparency seeds collaboration, output, and a healthy culture.

Our leadership hates politics. We want the best idea to win. We want a benevolent meritocracy. We see a tool like OKR as an enabler of that. It's not administrative busywork, it's an important way to set your priorities for the quarter and ensure alignment and transparency. As Daniel Pink says in *Drive*, the greatest single individual motivator is making progress in one's work. The simple act of writing a goal increases your chances of reaching it. The method fits with *Switch* and Simon Sinek's Golden Circle: you start an Objective with the inspirational *why* you're solving a

> The simple act of writing a goal increases your chances of reaching it.

specific issue. The days of "you'll do this because I said so" are over; people need to know why they are spending their time on something.

There is a wealth of tools available to facilitate OKR across the organization, including the one we adopted, called Gtm-hub. The web-based tools made it easy **People need to** to create goals and ensure transparent **know why they** visibility across the entire organization. **are spending** We could all see annual and quarter- **their time on** ly OKR from the highest level, with **something.** drill-down throughout the company.

Even with a proven process and great tools, it's still damned hard to create good OKR and make this an organizational habit. Your culture has to be right and supportive. Key Results are difficult for a lot of Objectives. In our first quarter or three, most of the KR were yes/no—did it get done or not. It's more difficult to find a great gauge you can look at to see where you stand on achievement without spending a lot of resources on building the gauge. An on/off gauge doesn't tell you much about progress. We found that a lot of metrics became an exercise in peeling back layers of the onion. We don't have an easy way to measure this because the process is broken, or we're not collecting that data, or we have no history/context. Good goals depend on good data. We all know how difficult it is to get good, clean data quickly.

Our first year of OKR was fraught with issues and shortcomings. It highlighted weaknesses in planning and execution. It pointed out issues with scoping, collecting metrics, and inefficient process. Any exercise that identifies weakness, issues, and inefficiency should be celebrated by the organization. Identifying and agreeing on the problem is the critical first step in creating a better future. OKR, like NPS, is a tried-and-true process supported with good tools. That doesn't make it *easy*; it makes it *easier*. Good goal setting is essential routine mainte-

Good goals depend on good data.

nance for thriving stakeholders. It may be the practice with the most immediate impact on all stakeholders. Without a good goal-setting process, you'll find things will continue breaking down, sometimes catastrophically.

You don't need your company to adopt OKR and tools to make it easy. You can start with just a quarterly set of written OKR for yourself. This could be personal or professional. It could be a set that is tied to an annual or five-year vision for you personally or for your group. If you want those to have a lot more power and accountability, share them. A small team could do this together, working from the goals that the leader has established for the group. Autonomy doesn't usually last long without accountability. Mastery isn't possible without goals and metrics. It should be natural for us as colleagues at work to want transparent and specific goals and metrics. As leaders we have to establish the right organizational conditions and practices to let this natural human need take hold and flourish.

Bringing It Home

Do you have a process for transparent goal setting at home?

What does it look like? I find that happening more often with a focus on the children's goals than the parents' goals. It might start with a list of chores. It often extends to school projects and grades, maybe because someone has already established a clear metric for measuring achievement. Then it it's college applications and résumés. Maybe throw in a little financial literacy. All of these are good muscles to exercise and they send your child off into the world with healthy habits for individual accountability, an understanding of mastery, and a healthy self-esteem. How often have you shared your goals as a parent? What would happen if you did?

TAKEAWAYS

- Thriving organizations figure out a way to set clear, meaningful, and measurable goals. This may be one of the hardest things for an organization to do well and is the most important "routine maintenance" a leader needs to establish.

- One reason this is hard is that people often want accountability for others—not themselves. People have to be encouraged to all be transparent about what they are specifically signing up to get done and how to measure what "done well" means.

- It is also difficult to avoid the trap of focusing goals on the daily tasks that each person is responsible for instead of identifying the few critical projects that need to be accomplished to drive the organization toward its vision; we have to avoid the temptation to mindlessly run on the treadmill of our daily tasks.

- OKR is a proven method for goal setting that has been adopted by many successful companies, including Intel and Google. It starts with a meaningful objective—akin to establishing a meaningful purpose that rallies an organization. The more challenging piece is setting measurable key results, because we are often lacking the data or systems we need to measure what we want.

- Goals are at the heart of human motivation. Autonomy and Mastery are impossible without strong goal-setting skills. Purpose is at the heart of good goal setting. Goals are like a regular oil change for the powerful engine of a motivated team.

QUESTIONS AND ACTIONS

- Do you resist transparent goals for yourself? Why?

- Think back to a time when you knew the powerful *why* behind what you were doing and what you were trying to accomplish. Do you have that at your current job? How does that feel?

- Think about a goal you've set for yourself

now. Have you written it down and shared
it with people who are close to you? If not,
why not? If so, do you think sharing your goal
with others makes it more likely that you will
succeed?

- Do you encourage your children to set goals?
  Do you share your own goals with them?

CHAPTER 17

REFLECTION

*Let's talk about a performance appraisal
that really means something.*

The Reflection is what we did to replace the traditional
Performance Appraisal with a self-appraisal aimed at
promoting a learning culture. I'm not sure we can talk
about a learning culture without confronting perfection and
self-esteem. So, before diving into what we did and how you
could do the same thing, I'd like to turn to Brené Brown and
her book *Daring Greatly*, which is inspired by a 1910 speech
from Theodore Roosevelt that ended up on our inspirational
quote wall in the office:

> It is not the critic who counts; not the man who
> points out how the strong man stumbles, or where
> the doer of deeds could have done them better.

The credit belongs to the man who is actually in the arena, whose face is marred by dust and sweat and blood; who strives valiantly; who errs, who comes short again and again,

Because there is no effort without error and shortcoming; but who does actually strive to do the deeds; who knows great enthusiasms, the great devotions; who spends himself in a worthy cause;

Who at the best knows in the end the triumph of high achievement, and who at the worst, if he fails, at least fails while daring greatly.[75]

The most excruciating moments of my professional career occurred when we saw someone with incredible potential who would not join us in the arena. If you'll come onto the field and play the game, I'm sure we can work this out together. If you won't be part of the solution, we can't play. If you want to stay in the stands and criticize without taking any chances of your own, the game is over. I've challenged many people to join us on the field. The ones who refuse are painful; for whatever reason, they won't engage, they simply want to complain about how things are not the way they should be or the way they want them to be. We may fail, we may be bloody, it may be exhausting and painful, but if you'll come onto the field and give it your all, I'll be right there beside you.

A traditional appraisal feels like I'm sitting in the stands and criticizing everything you did in the last year. I wasn't often on the field with you. I was more often trying to impress my boss and move up. And that might include me finding reasons why you shouldn't get more money, so I could come in under budget. I've been told to come up with a numeric rating of your performance and fit it within an arbitrary bell curve. We are clearly on opposite sides of a zero-sum negotiating table. Can I honestly expect you to dare greatly?

> When we spend our lives waiting until we're perfect or bulletproof before we walk into the arena, we ultimately sacrifice relationships and opportunities that may not be recoverable, we squander our precious time, and we turn our backs on our gifts. . . . *Perfect* and *bulletproof* are seductive, but they don't exist in the human experience. . . . Rather than sitting on the sidelines and hurling judgment and advice, **we must dare to show up and let ourselves be seen.**[76]

As leaders, how do we help create the right environment for our people to get off the sidelines and join us in the game? It would seem highly improbable to expect that to happen optimally in a traditional work environment where human resources are fed into the profit machine. Or when nobody understands the rules of the game we're playing. Or when management and employee operate as opposing forces in a zero-sum game. Or when perfection, and

> As leaders, how do we help create the right environment for our people to get off the sidelines and join us in the game?

its partner-in-crime, shame, end up ruling the roost.

Every time someone holds back on a new idea, fails to give their manager much needed feedback, and is afraid to speak up in front of a client, you can be sure shame played a part. That deep fear we have of being wrong, of being belittled, of feeling less than enough, is what stops us from taking the very risks required to move our companies forward.[77]

So, an organization led by perfectionists is likely to be very challenging for people. If those leaders are high performing and rarely if ever seem to fail or never acknowledge failing, the myth of perfection becomes truth. Couple that with the necessity of measuring and driving performance and productivity in business, and there is likely to be a naturally challenging environment for people to dare greatly. Throw on top of that my belief that many people were raised in shaming environments, many people do not have a healthy and resilient sense of self-worth, and many

It is essential for the culture of an organization to stamp out shame, blame, and perhaps (gasp!) comparison.

people have worked in unhealthy cultures focused on profit and the myth of the perfect leader. Add that increased fear when you are "creating" in your job, whether it be code, designs, process, words, ideas, etc. It should come as no surprise that people keep their heads low, are slow to trust, do not naturally want to take risks. How then do we combat this and thoughtfully create a culture to counter this while still measuring our individual and team contributions?

It seems all the more important to patiently assemble the blocks of trust, for leaders to demonstrate humanity and vulnerability. It is essential for the culture of an organization to stamp out shame, blame, and perhaps (gasp!) comparison. The trick is to do all that while measuring performance and driving accountability. It shines a light on the importance of discovering the unique strengths and gifts of the team and develop those.

Traditional appraisals are one-way streets; they're something that happens *to* an employee, it's not a collaborative discussion. They're not a learning exercise. I appraise you and I'm not really looking for you to provide me feedback. I'm certainly not going to share my own appraisal with you. We're likely to spend our time working on fixing your weaknesses rather than honing your strengths.

Good leaders should feel accountable to the team for their performance. Of course, the team is accountable to them as the manager. But how often does the leader feel accountable to the team for their own performance? To help us begin the transformation from "appraisal" to "reflection," we felt we needed to back our words with action and share our own reflections with the entire team. What better way to establish our own vulnerability and imperfection?

Thankfully, our culture demands humility, especially in leaders. A true servant leader must be humble. This is yet another thing that we felt in our gut rather than something we researched and intentionally sought out. We found lots of supporting research later. In *Humble Inquiry*, Edgar Schein writes that humility in leadership can literally be the difference between life and death. What he defines as Here-and-now Humility "is often totally invisible to the boss who may assume that the formal power granted by the position itself will guarantee the performance of a subordinate."[78]

If you are not demonstrating humility and building trust, you are likely to find yourself missing information you need to make critical decisions. As a leader, there are already a host of barriers that prevent people from offering honest information. You have to work to create the conditions that make it possible for it to flow to you. If you think that you're perfect, you are highly unlikely to seek it out, and you'll unconsciously build even higher barriers to that information reaching you.

This is not to say that our leaders don't struggle with perfection. I do, and many of our other leaders do as well. We struggle with expecting perfection from ourselves, not from others. We torture ourselves for our failures. We desperately don't want to let our team down or commit mistakes that can endanger them. Our self-appraisals are more critical than any traditional appraisal would be, so I wasn't too worried about our top leaders being honest about their shortcomings.

In chapter 9 on Compensation, I discussed scale bias and how we realized that it was impossible for us to use a performance number from the appraisal to establish compensation. Letting go of that fallacy made it easier for us to transition appraisal into reflection. Sharing our own failures as leaders helps erode the myth of perfection. Eventually the team (grudgingly) agreed that we were not pulling a fast one—we were not asking them to appraise themselves in some double-secret attempt to translate a performance number into compensation. We truly were seeking learning and feedback and asking them to join us in the arena.

Still, it has been difficult to drive the Reflection where it needs to go. We have to remember that we have inherited most of our team from other places, and they arrive with organizational baggage that is very difficult to unpack. They arrive with brains largely wired in their teens and from all sorts of upbringings, many of which did not produce healthy self-esteem and positivity. The decision to dump the annual appraisal in favor for a self-assessment was easy. The structure of it is easy. It takes no more time than a traditional appraisal. It can be done at any time during the year and more often than annually. With regular Check-ins, there are notes and data to feed the Reflection. The responsibility for drafting the reflection is where it should be: on the colleague seeking to learn and grow from looking back on the past thoughtfully and honestly. The form is straightforward, and as with NPS, the score isn't the point. The Position Alignment provides you with a clear description of your responsibilities. Anyone who gives an honest effort on the Reflection can feel that sense of freedom and peace you get when you step off the treadmill for a few moments and just think.

It will take our organization some time before all of our team lets go of the traditional approach and genuinely looks back with the goal of learning how to become better. Letting

> Sharing our own failures as leaders helps erode the myth of perfection.

go of perfection is difficult. So is showing vulnerability. So is having the courage to provide honest feedback to your manager and the company. So is digging around in your Position Alignment to find your gifts. We will never get to Reflection nirvana: Reflection perfection. At least we are in the arena, trying.

It's more difficult to provide an example Reflection for you to follow. Each reflection will include a lot of company-specific lingo and acronyms. Good Reflections will contain a lot of specifics about our business—quite a bit of confidential information that we wouldn't want in the public domain. Our initial Reflection invites each team member to do a SWOT analysis (Strengths, Weaknesses, Opportunities, and Threats). We don't care what level they do this on; it can be in their group, department, division, and/or on the company as a whole. We're again inviting our colleagues to join us on the same side of the table and honestly assess where we sit as if it were coming from an outside consultant, a competitor, or a board member. I've tried to genericize one of mine in hopes that it can function as a basic example without revealing anything confidential. I think the sanitization neuters the example, but I'm hopeful that it will be better than starting from a blank sheet of paper. Our current Reflection form is also in appendix 4, and you will find it is much less daunting.

While we encourage publicizing Reflections, we certainly recognize that there are many things that are confidential and cannot be shared with everyone. As the CEO, I found there were a host of things that I reflected on that I couldn't share completely with the team without breaking confidentiality. I couldn't talk about a failed acquisition. I wasn't ready to discuss my transition out of the business. I didn't want to discuss issues within our leadership team while still trying to resolve them. It's okay for me to have one Reflection that I share with only my manager that is complete, while sharing an edited version with the entire team. They can certainly get the gist of my accomplishments without the details behind all of them. The main thing is that I'm practicing what we preach, demonstrating imperfection, and showing that, in the end, I serve the team at their pleasure and at the pleasure of the owners. I'm genuinely trying to assess my own performance, build some confidence from the wins, gain a better understanding of my talents, assess my weaknesses, and learn from failures. This is for me first and foremost, aimed at creating that next great version of me. My manager is my coach and should be holding me accountable—not to a score, but to ensure I'm being honest and fair with myself.

Most of my team members are harder on themselves than they should be. My job as coach is to help them stop beating themselves up and encourage them to let go of perfection while still holding themselves to a high standard. My job is to help guide them down the road of their own talents and help them find partners to uncover blind spots and balance them out. It's to help them assess their own teams and hold them accountable to the goals they've committed to achieving. It becomes a very different session, where I'm not being asked to fit an arbitrary score to a bell curve by myself. It's not my responsibility to point out all the things you need to fix to be a more perfect human resource. As a manager, this becomes something that I look forward to instead of a dreaded duty. I'm editing; I'm not drafting ten or twenty of these things for HR to put into a file folder. The onus for a colleague's growth is where it should be: on the colleague. After all, you are a trusted adult and should be expected to be able to complete an assessment of yourself. Why would you want to delegate that to someone who isn't there for a lot of what you did?

This is clearly something that you can practice no matter where you are in the organization. When you're forced to sit down and fill out the annual performance appraisal for your company, you could consider whether to use that as an opportunity to reflect back honestly. Whether you put any of that content into your appraisal is your decision. The goal is to step off the treadmill and honestly assess how you did without anyone looking over your shoulder. How did you mess up, and what did you learn from that? Where did you shine, and what does that say about your talents, which ultimately has something to say about your happiness? If you've created your own Position Alignment, where are the opportunities for mastery and developing the next great version of you? This reflection gives you a pretty good picture of where you are now, so you can use this as the foundation of mapping where you want to be a year from now. If you are a manager of a team, you could encourage your team members to take a more active role in the appraisal and in using this time to reflect—whether they choose to share that reflection with you or not.

Bringing It Home

For most families, it seems like the nearest thing to an appraisal is the report card process. How else does a child get regular feedback? Could these events become an opportunity to help look more closely at past performance, both within and beyond the school day? Does this more regular coaching provide an opportunity for more feedback, recognition, gratitude, and relationship building? Does it help encourage a lifetime habit of reflection that spurs learning and development? I haven't spoken directly to Younger Me very much in this section. Reflecting on Reflection, this is something I wish that I would have applied more at home.

I cannot think of a good reason to do a traditional annual performance appraisal. The decision to move to a Reflection is easy and the process is straightforward, with a lot fewer organizational roadblocks and disruption. The hard part is reframing the purpose, letting go of perfection and power and shame, and letting ourselves take time off the treadmill to reflect on how we can be better. Many people will likely have a hard time moving away from a formal assessment of performance with a number attached to it. I suggest that a good goal-setting process should make that concern evaporate, as well as an intentional talent review and compensation process.

TAKEAWAYS

- The Reflection turns the dreaded performance

appraisal into an exercise of learning, discovery, and development. It helps break down the myth of perfection and encourage vulnerability, which enables the flow of valuable information that just might save your company.

- Our Reflection is a self-appraisal. You rate your own performance solely for your own comparison. Scale bias, poor record-keeping, and a narrow view of an individual's performance make it nearly impossible to assign a fair numeric ranking to an annual appraisal.

- Many factors beyond an organization's control conspire to prevent team members from joining together on the field to take risks and expend maximum voluntary effort. A leader needs to carefully design the conditions that allow team members to "dare greatly."

- Reflection is an essential ingredient to a learning culture. Leaders can demonstrate vulnerability, transparency, and learning by sharing their own honest reflections on performance. This sets an example for others to follow and encourages others to take initiative and let go of fear.

- The Position Alignment helps an individual reflect on performance in each key area of responsibility. Regular Check-ins provide a record of achievement and learning that help ensure a self-appraisal is fact-based. Good goal setting helps provide data to support assessment.

- Anyone can do an honest reflection—it doesn't have to be part of your organization's process. Once or twice annually, give yourself the gift of looking back honestly at where you've been, where you are now, and where you want to be.

QUESTIONS AND ACTIONS

- Reflect back on the last year honestly. Give yourself a score in each area of responsibility, both at work and at home. What's your own scale bias?

- Think about the best manager you've ever had. How did she assess your performance? Was that a big part of why you felt this manager was so good?

- What could you do to help your annual appraisal be more like a two-way learning exercise?

- Think for a moment about who is ultimately in control of your own learning and development.

- Take a moment and think about the strengths, weaknesses, opportunities, and threats that you see in the organization you are part of today. Are you more or less optimistic about the future? Could you do the same assessment about yourself or your family?

CHAPTER 18

DEVELOPMENT

What does the next great version of you look like?

M ost traditional appraisals have a section about professional development. In the traditional annual appraisal,
most of the time allotted is devoted to talking about
weaknesses and how to improve on them. Before I became
responsible for an organization, I had eight managers in my
working career. I can't recall more than a moment or two of
time with my managers that was focused on what I did well.
As a manager within these corporations, I don't recall any
training about delivering performance appraisals, and certainly there were no instructions to focus on strengths, so I largely
followed the examples of managers before me and spent my
time focused on weaknesses.

Marcus Buckingham and Curt Coffman's book *First,
Break All the Rules* changed that for me. As an engineer, of
course I was drawn to the data; over a million interviews and

five million pages of transcripts made an impression. While that appealed to the head, there was plenty that reached my heart and my gut. The authors advised that great managers don't waste time trying to put in what was left out; instead, they work to draw out the gifts inside. It made sense that focusing on strengths would be more efficient than trying to fix long-standing weaknesses. It meant focusing on the positive and avoiding the baggage of expecting perfection from others. And it fit with what I had seen in the trenches: people will be more open to improvements when they are working from a solid foundation of appreciation and an understanding of the value they contribute.

> People will be more open to improvements when they are working from a solid foundation of appreciation and an understanding of the value they contribute.

I think the most difficult challenge we face in business is finding talent. The interview process is time-consuming and flawed. Great working environments depend on relationships, those relationships take time to develop, and the interview process is like speed-dating. Even if you do ten hours of interviews before making an offer, the process is tainted on both ends. It's tainted by hiring managers relying on their own biases and praying for a quick and miraculous end to the process so they can get back on the treadmill. It's tainted by applicants who are on their best behavior and almost always driven by a single goal: the offer.

We do our best to encourage a two-way conversation to ensure this is a good long-term match. We want applicants to interview the company too; otherwise, it feels like all they want is a warm body instead of a lifelong partner. As I've mentioned previously, in many hours of interviews, I have not met anyone who can honestly and concisely articulate their values, strengths, and weaknesses. Given the focus on discussing weaknesses and an overall dearth of genuine and specific gratitude in most workplaces, this shouldn't be surprising. But it does make it very difficult to find the right talent.

If an individual's brain has been wired for virtually all of its important connections by the time a person is in his teens, as Buckingham and Coffman assert, then they show up for the interview with a set of talents. If you're diligent, you have about ten hours of interviewing to figure out what those are and whether they fit the role. It's doubtful you'll get quick and easy answers from the candidate, so you'll have to dig around carefully. And you also have to figure out their values and whether they are compatible with yours. This feels like proposing marriage after three dates.

Buckingham and Coffman list Selecting Talent as one of the four things that great managers do well. They provide some guidance around distinguishing talents from skills. And they acknowledge that it is hard to select for talent because few people know what their talents are. Someday, we will develop a better process. As more businesses work with people to clearly identify and develop talents, more people will arrive at an interview with a clear description of what those talents are and why they fit the responsibilities of the role. Who knows, maybe résumés will do a better job of clearly identifying your gifts, complete with examples of how you applied them for the greater good, and we can spend our time talking about whether those gifts well and truly fit the job we have to offer. That would mean more to me than a list of the places you worked and the titles you held.

So, we do the best we can in the process we have because it doesn't seem like we've found a better way. And now that person is part of our family and the relationship building really begins. And it becomes our jobs as leaders to help "draw out what's been left in."

Again, saddled with a New York upbringing, it's difficult for me to avoid focusing on what's been left out. As an engineer, I solve problems, and weaknesses are problems to be fixed. If nothing else, the book *First, Break All the Rules* reminded me to search for the gifts in people and stop worrying about what's not there. The problem is reframed: instead of thinking of the problem as fixing weaknesses, the problem becomes finding out what the strengths are and how to apply them.

> Search for the gifts in people and stop worrying about what's not there.

Recognizing weaknesses should be a road to finding ways to work around them and not for complaining about why that person can't be the person we want them to be. When I found myself complaining about a long-time colleague, one of my peers reminded me to stop worrying about what was left out and be thankful for what that colleague did well. Tendencies and organizational baggage drag us toward the traditional. We need to train each other on the right path so that we can work together as a group and hold each other accountable to the positive path. This was one reason *First, Break All the Rules* became a pillar of our leadership training.

Accepting that weaknesses may be baked into a person's brain does not mean ignoring poor performance. Buckingham and Coffman point out that great managers know this: "Poor performance must confronted head-on and quickly. Most poor performance is caused by not having the tools or information needed to do the job or because the employee is dealing with a personal crisis."[79] This is another reason why the Check-in is so valuable: it encourages regular, respectful, two-way feedback about performance. It puts the onus on the colleague to raise issues about a lack of resources, tools, information, and other eminently solvable roadblocks. Asking me as the manager and you as the colleague to fix something that was baked into your head by the time you were fourteen is not something we're going to nail. Let's work together on something worthwhile.

If there is a weakness you're just not wired for, there are other ways to address it besides getting you to the point where you suck a little less. We could find someone else to partner with you who is great at what you're not great at. We could restructure your responsibilities so you do less of that. I could take that in exchange for you taking something I'm not good at. The trick is developing the relationship so we can talk about it without getting defensive or defining you. Knowing that you have demonstrated gifts makes it a little easier to admit that you aren't great at everything.

The Check-in sets the stage for the real work of Development: helping people become better versions of themselves.

That phrase alone, "creating better versions of yourself," is a positive and enabling way of thinking about feedback. I'm not criticizing the way you are built inside or who you are as a person. Most of our discussion and time together is spent identifying the features of you that are wonderful and what the organization values and loves about you. Feedback is aimed at addressing the bugs in your code (or "undocumented features," if you're speaking to a programmer). What's inherent in your design that creates usability or reliability issues? How do we work around those? What new features does your design enable?

> The Check-in sets the stage for the real work of Development: helping people become better versions of themselves.

I'm not trying to dehumanize people. This analogy can obviously be taken too far. But the analogy holds even if you are not in the software business. We all use software applications. We all have favorites for certain functions. We all see that new versions come along all the time and make our lives even better. Thinking about "better versions" makes it less of a personal criticism. It is forward-looking and hopeful. It acknowledges that the current version is pretty darned amazing already. It recognizes things can always be better but will never be perfect. Our goal together is not to create the perfect employee or even the perfect you. Perfection is a trap and a myth. Our goal is to work together to discover what wonders lurk inside of you, what wiring holds you back, and to map out a realistic plan for the next great release of you. Not just because that will make the organization more money (it probably will). Because it will make you happier, more productive, more engaged, less willing to leave, and a better colleague all around. And better at home. Helping people create better versions of themselves is a win-win, or as they'd say in Texas: winner, winner, chicken dinner. Learning and improvement is essential to thriving.

The Development section of the 1-2-1 is aimed at uncovering your colleague's unique gifts. What was wired into that brain before it arrived on your doorstop? What specific quantitative and qualitative data have we gathered together that helps identify those talents? I contend that if you can do this for just one of your people, then you will be fondly remembered as having a positive impact on that person's life beyond just a paycheck. This doesn't have to be an authorized process from your HR department for you to try it. If you're nervous about it, try tackling this exercise on the one person you will always be the boss of: yourself.

> Our goal is to work together to discover what wonders lurk inside of you, what wiring holds you back, and to map out a realistic plan for the next great release of you.

And now onto the taboo part of the Development section: the paycheck. Are you comfortable talking to your manager about your pay? If you are, then I believe you are a unicorn—according to a survey by Total Jobs, two-thirds of respondents said they were not comfortable discussing their salary or asking for a pay raise.[80] For most people, this conversation is highly uncomfortable. What I think goes on in most people's head is: "My manager and the company should really know what I'm worth. If they don't give me what I think is fair, it means they really don't care or recognize what I bring to the table."

Well, what if they really *don't* know what you're worth? It's not that straightforward to figure out. Remember, there's no price tag stamped on your forehead. There are flawed salary surveys, unclear value of benefits, working environment, quality of your manager and leadership, your starting compensation, your increases, and what other people are earning for similar value and responsibilities. Some of that is quantitative, but the data is messy. What's fair? And why can't we have an open and respectful discussion about these questions?

Not having this kind of conversation opens us up to a surprise. In business and in life, bad surprises are stressful and often avoidable. As a manager, one of your most difficult days is when a valued colleague hands you a surprise resignation. The shock and pain arrive in waves and last for weeks or months. Compensation is only one reason that may happen, but it's very important to people, so why can't we have discussion about it before the surprise happens? If the relationship is strong enough, people will give you the chance to discuss it. If you respond with defensiveness or anger, word gets around. If you show that it's okay to talk about what's important to you, then you've got a better chance at getting onto the same side of the table instead of packing up and saying goodbye.

The Talent Review process helped us with this. At least each colleague knows that there is a thoughtful process and they see company-wide data about the increases given versus the standard. Total Compensation Statements help by providing data about what else goes into compensation beyond salary. Notes from regular Check-ins help. As usual, data can help form a less emotional foundation for discussion about how you are compensated for the work you do. While you may have to talk about the quality of the data, at least you're looking for facts together.

Mostly, though, the Development section is meant to be the design session for the next great version of you. And this is not easy. You don't come with a price tag, and you also don't come with a detailed design guide from your manufacturer. Your User Manual may provide some qualitative hints about how your brain is wired. Where else can we look besides experiences?

There are plenty of tools out there that can help. Buckingham and Coffman followed up with some practical guidance in their book *Now, Discover Your Strengths*. Many people have used the Myers-Briggs assessments or other such tools. One tool that I found helpful was the Reflected Best Self Exercise. In the RBSE, I asked people who knew me very well to tell me three stories about when they saw me at my best. Asking people to tell you stories is much easier than asking them what your talents are. The tricky part is pulling out specific talents from the stories. Even if that proves difficult, reading the stories is a confidence builder. I recently took a Birkman test and found it to be eerily accurate. If you're having trouble doing this on your own, there's lots of help out there.

You just might become that leader someone remembers forever for helping change a life.

No matter where you are in the organization, helping articulate talents is something you can do without permission. Focusing more on drawing what lies within instead of adding what's been left out will lower your stress. It will improve your relationships with your coworkers if you are honestly and specifically identifying innate talents instead of focusing on why your colleague is a jerk. And you just might become that leader someone remembers forever for helping change a life. It's not easy to do. It is worthwhile.

Bringing It Home

In *First, Break All the Rules*, Buckingham and Coffman assert that people's brains are largely developed relatively early in life. People end up with innate "superhighways and footpaths"— wiring in the brain that makes some things much easier and other things much harder. Call them God's gifts, talents, or whatever you like. One of a parent's jobs should be to help identify those superhighways in the brain. Would your life have been different if your parents sent you away to college with a list of what they thought you were great at? Most people leave home more aware of what they don't do well than what they are great at. Maybe we can look for the things our children spend the most time on. Look for the things to draw out rather than focusing on what's been left out. When was the last time your spouse recognized what you were amazing at? (Other than your ability to completely ignore a full trash can,

People rarely love to do something that they stink at.

full hamper, or full dishwasher.) When is the last time you looked at your spouse and appreciated how his or her strengths balance out the "footpaths" in your brain?

Your talents will likely reveal themselves when you are doing what you love to do. People rarely love to do something that they stink at.

TAKEAWAYS

- Development is the plan for creating the next great version of you. It starts with a focus on the positive and dealing with the negative from a position of confidence and mutual respect. Routinely engaging in Development tunes the organization and drives performance.
- If it is true that the human brain is largely wired by the time we're in our teens, then it's a waste of energy to focus on a person's weaknesses. Instead of focusing on what's been left out of a colleague, let's focus on discovering the amazing talents that often lay hidden.
- Positive practices that help identify strengths include the Position Alignment, Check-ins, User Manual, goal setting and Reflection. All of these provide data and experiences that we can look at together to clarify what makes you wonderful and how we can create the next great version of you.
- A regular discussion about your development should include an honest discussion about what is

traditionally an uncomfortable subject: compensation. An honest discussion about this helps build trust and prevent surprise resignations.

- Starting with a focus on strengths builds the confidence to address weaknesses and the many ways we can minimize their impact on your performance. A leader or colleague who can help someone clearly understand their talents will be remembered fondly.

QUESTIONS AND ACTIONS

- Prepare your own honest response to the question "What are my strengths and weaknesses?" Can you rewrite your résumé to highlight your strengths and support them with examples and data?

- If, when you left home, your parents wrote you a letter describing what they saw as your strengths, what do you think they would have said? If you have children, what would you tell them?

- What does the next great version of you look like? What features do you want to add and what bugs do you want to resolve?

- What do you think you are worth? What data do you have to back that up?

- Think for a moment about the things that you love to do. When time flies by before you know it, what are you doing? What is it about you that draws you to that activity?

- What are you terrible at doing? Who can you partner with that might balance you?

CONCLUSION

Business is bad. Ask most people and they will agree. Business is part of the problem in our society, not part of the solution. Ask your friends and family and you will likely hear plenty of horror stories about the working world. Read the news and you'll likely find a story about the bad behavior of business leadership. Being part of the business world is, for many people, a necessary evil. We've all got bills to pay. Too often, business doesn't offer us the joy of productive contribution and growth.

Sadly, the prevailing definition of the purpose of business is from the 1970s: make the most money you can within the confines of the law. Oh, and somehow there are folks who forget about that last part. Over and over, companies demonstrate a preference for adhering to the letter of the law in their aim to drive profit over any moral responsibility to employees, customers, suppliers, or the community. And sometimes also without regard for the shareholders. According to the consulting firm Deloitte, 80 percent of people are dissatisfied with their jobs.[81]

Business is also a powerful force for good. More and more businesses are realizing that they can do the right thing *and* make money. Research shows that thriving businesses actually make more money. *Conscious Capitalism* includes an entire appendix on this. "A representative sample of conscious firms outperformed the overall stock market by a ratio of 10.5:1 over a fifteen-year period."[82] What Mackey and Sisodia call "conscious," I call thriving—businesses that intentionally and diligently strive to have a positive impact on *all stakeholders*. *Share*holders should be just one *stake*holder in a business. Employees, customers, suppliers, and the community should be considered on the same footing as shareholders. Companies that focus only on profit are failing our society in many ways. Thankfully, the tide is changing, and more companies are actively working to create a thriving workplace.

Mackey and Sisodia cite an important reframing for business. Instead of business—and by implication its stakeholders—being greedy and exploitative, the true nature of business is that it creates prosperity, lifts people out of poverty, creates stable conditions for families to be raised, and helps build strong communities. Business creates places for people to exchange value, find meaning, build important relationships, and belong. "When people realize that they are part of the largest force for positive social transformation in history, their self-perception changes."[83]

We are at a tipping point in how we define the purpose

of business. That definition from the 1970s is still the majority view. Serving five stakeholders is much more difficult than serving one. And making a profit is difficult enough as it is. The economist N. Gregory Mankiw tackled this subject in a *New York Times* article published July 26, 2020. In it, he quotes Joe Biden as saying: "It's way past time we put an end to the era of shareholder capitalism, the idea the only responsibility a corporation has is with shareholders. That's simply not true. . . . They have a responsibility to their workers, their community, to their country."[84] Mankiw points out that "in forsaking a mandate of narrow self-interest for one of broad social welfare, this approach to corporate management sounds noble, perhaps even obvious. But it is more problematic under closer scrutiny."

He outlines a number of very difficult questions of balance that would be faced by leadership seeking to serve more than profit. He contends, "this approach to corporate management expects executives to be broadly competent social planners rather than narrowly focused profit maximizers. It's unlikely that corporate executives, with their business training and limited experience, have the skills to play this role well."

As a CEO, I always felt I didn't have enough expertise. I was constantly moving across the breadth of the organization with broad and shallow knowledge. I'm not trained as an attorney, but I had to make a lot of legal decisions and work my way through a lot of contracts. I did that with the help of outside and inside experts. I'm not an electrical engineer or a programmer, so I had to make sure we had that expertise and someone capable of helping me understand enough about the subjects to make good decisions. I'm not an auditor, CPA, salesperson, marketer, and on and on. In fact, I bet that most business leaders do not have deep expertise in many areas. I didn't study profit maximizing in business school, though after twenty-five years, one thing I'm sure about is there is nothing narrow about the focus areas in which a CEO is expected to be well-versed so they can maximize profit.

Mankiw concludes his article by writing, ". . . the world needs people to look out for the broad well-being of society. But those people are not corporate executives. They are elected leaders who are competent and trustworthy. Sadly, we have not had such leadership . . ."

I believe the problems that we face are too big to wait for the government to make them all go away. They're too much for us unless we all pull together and do our part. The government is not going to save us. Leaders must find a way to make the economic pie bigger and to share it more equitably. Positive leadership practices can address societal problems *and* deliver strong financial results.

In her 2020 book *Think Outside the Building*, Rosabeth Moss Kanter writes, "Big systems problems spill across sectors, and they land in different places depending on the setting. . . . There are no rules defining who can solve problems and the sector from which they emanate. For-profit, not-for-profit or public section actions and solutions can be involved."[85] In 1969, the government put people on the moon. Now, it is Elon Musk and his SpaceX that's launching people into space. Companies that once had an "allegiance only to shareholders and profits" are now pressured by the public to take greater responsibility and "embrace multiple stakeholders, not just investors, and even to get involved in making the wider world a better place."[86] Kanter agrees with Mankiw that this is a very difficult task for business.

Business cannot solve all of our big problems, certainly not by itself, nor am I advocating that. My point is that our issues have become too big for us to wait for government, non-profits, and individuals to address them. Business can be, and must be, part of the solution. If nothing else, business could make quite a dent in things just by not creating more problems or exacerbating the ones we have. This is something I wish Younger Me was encouraged to consider. Stop thinking just about profit, and start thinking about how you, as a business leader, can make things better *and* make a profit too.

In his book *Leaders Eat Last*, Simon Sinek writes:

> A business environment with an unbalanced short-term focus on results and money before people affects society at large. When we struggle to find happiness or a sense of belonging at work, we take that struggle home. Those who have an opportunity to work in organizations that treat them like human beings to be protected rather than a resource to be exploited come home at the end of the day with an intense feeling of fulfillment and gratitude. This should be the rule of the day for all of us, not the exception. Returning from work feeling inspired, safe,

fulfilled, and grateful is a natural human right to which we are all entitled and not a modern luxury that only a few lucky ones are able to find.[87]

Our sense of right or wrong, despite the letter of the law, matters on a social level. This is the very foundation of civil society. Being a company of high moral standard is the same as being a person of high moral character—a standard not easily determined by the law, but easily recognized by anyone. We need to build more organizations that prioritize the care of human beings. As leaders, it is our responsibility to protect our people, and, in turn, our people will protect each other and advance the organization together. It is our responsibility to do right by our employees, customers, suppliers, and communities, as well as our shareholders.

> As leaders, it is our responsibility to protect our people, and, in turn, our people will protect each other and advance the organization together.

The techniques of positive leadership not only impact society—they are not just soft skills that make the world a better place—they result in better performance. We need to reverse the damaging effects of prioritizing money, status, and power. We need to update the purpose of business to include a responsibility to all stakeholders. We need to do what is right.

Thriving organizations:

- Have more engaged people who drive better results.

- Are more sustainable in a competitive and rapidly changing world.

- Create jobs that help people learn, grow, and contribute to the betterment of their organizations, families, and communities.

- Foster high-quality relationships across economic, ethnic, gender, and social differences.

- Actively look for ways to help people become the best versions of themselves.

- Are an essential foundation to a positive and thriving society.

Thriving organizations will also keep our leaders sane and prevent them from burning out. Great leaders genuinely care about all of their stakeholders. Leading a toxic organization is soul-crushing and abhorrent to any decent human being. I was astonished at some of the things I encountered in my time leading an organization. I was sorely tempted on many occasions to react by emulating many of the big corporations I worked for: go into lockdown, catch the criminals, and trust nobody. All of us have had someone betray our trust at some point in our lives. Our initial reaction to heartbreak is to say, "Well, I'm not going to trust anyone anymore so I don't get hurt like that again."

Then you realize that life in emotional lockdown, without trust and meaningful relationships, is worse than any heartbreak. That's what drew me to look for positive business practices; I didn't want to live in one of the toxic cultures I encountered in my past and I certainly didn't want to lead an organization that eliminated joy, love, and human connection from the working day.

What I soon realized is that a positive and thriving culture is a wonderful place for a good leader. It doesn't guarantee that nobody will betray your trust. But it does dramatically reduce the probability that will happen. And it results in many more moments of joy. It provides a lot more energy than it sucks away from you. It means less time on crisis, repairs, and defense. It means more time on offense, improvement, learning, and growth. Great leaders are servant leaders. But for just one moment, I'd encourage you do to this for yourself if not for the organization.

One of the most impactful things business and leaders can do for people is to help them grow. Creating a thriving organization builds trust and belief that people can change for the better. And in time, people begin to believe that the workplace can be an engaging place of mutual benefit. A job can help pay your bills. A thriving workplace does that while helping you discover your own gifts and face your own shortcomings with honesty and support. Human resources can feed the profit machine, but a thriving workplace creates engaged people and results in a lot less bad behavior.

In our leadership training, we often begin by asking people to think about the worst leader they've ever had. Listening to them talk, you can hear the damage done by those leaders, and the pain and frustration are still fresh. We then ask them to think about the best leader they've come across. The love and admiration are as fresh as ever, and people bask in the memories. We then ask them what kind of leader they want to be remembered as.

I was lucky to work with owners who encouraged our work and allowed us to experiment with many different practices for more than twenty-five years. Our business is still on its journey to build a high-performing organization that brings out the best in people. We continue to study what other people are doing, we try out interesting ideas, and we share our experiences with others. We regularly interact with like-minded organizations to network, share ideas, and support each other.

It's hard to run a growing and consistently profitable business. It's even harder to be accountable to five stakeholders—customers, employees, suppliers, communities, and shareholders—to measure the organization's success against more than the bottom line. But the payoff is big. Society needs business to do more than make money, just as we need to actively address equity and inclusion instead of just following the letter of the law or comfortable societal norms. Very few worthy efforts are easy.

I started this book by putting words into my dad's mouth. He was born in 1927, two years before the Great Depression started. His parents divorced when he was in his teens. He was eighteen when World War II ended. His dad died before he graduated from college. His childhood was not an easy life. He was a hard worker and could endure any hardship thrown his way (even six sons). A job meant security and a way to feed his family. For him, that was plenty. He worked for the same company in the same location for fifty years. I don't think he ever expected business to do anything more than help him provide for his family.

In his lifetime, he increasingly complained about how the government wasn't meeting his expectations. The New Deal, a man on the moon, the Civil Rights Act . . . those turned into Watergate, wealth disparity, mass incarceration. The world is a very different place today—in many positive and negative ways. Generations of workers are entering business with very different expectations than my dad had. Governments everywhere are straining to stay within sight of the needs of their people. Business cannot afford to limit itself to making money for investors and providing people with a job. And that's not even a choice we have to make as leaders, since thriving organizations are more successful. The tide is clearly turning. Coincidentally, Milton Friedman established his narrow definition of business in 1970, at the same time as Robert Greenleaf introduced us to servant leadership. I think my dad would be ecstatic that his granddaughters are more likely to work for business leaders who choose to take the harder and more meaningful path instead of a limited and singular focus on money.

I'll let Simon Sinek have the last word here: "Leadership is not a license to do less; it is a responsibility to do more. . . . Leadership takes work. The effects are not always easily measured and not often immediate. Leadership is always a commitment to human beings."[88]

ACKNOWLEDGMENTS

I am grateful to all of my colleagues at American Innovations for their dedication and support throughout my time learning how to be a better leader. I was blessed to have had the privilege of working with owners who were patient and recognized that true success is creating value for all of an organization's stakeholders. I learned from so many great leaders in YEO and YPO and I'm particularly grateful for all of the forum mates that I had along the way. I learned so much from all of the amazing authors who appear in this book – you have touched so many leaders like me and I hope that I've represented you well in this story. I also want to express my thanks to all of the people who provided valuable feedback to me along the way and especially the team at Content Capital and to Wayne Baker. Last but not least, I am eternally grateful to my wife Anne for her unrelenting optimism and encouragement, and for showing me what true love and great leadership look like every day.

1-2-1 CHECK-IN AGENDA

1-2-1 CHECK-IN AGENDA

Role Negotiation

- Review your Position Alignments before your first meeting and prepare your questions.
- Discuss each other's Position Alignments.
  - Are roles and responsibilities clear?
  - Does the time allotted seem reasonable?
  - What portions of your responsibilities most interest you?
  - How do you see this role changing over time to best suit you?

First Meeting

- Make it clear that the Check-in should benefit both parties and that our goal is to build mutual respect and work together on problems.
- Create a Teams Group for each 1-2-1 direct report and add a Notebook to keep notes—this way

both manager and direct report can see and edit meeting notes.

- Discuss how you like to be recognized and rewarded. In public or private? What are things that you like to do that might inform non-monetary thanks you will appreciate?
- Discuss expectations for these meetings and how often you want to do them.
- Discuss who will create the 1-2-1 meeting invites—onus is on the employee.
- Discuss salary expectations, talent review, and compensation planning—make sure that compensation is something that we can openly discuss together.

Agenda Topic Ideas

- Gratitude Opener: start with something positive about what's been going well, acknowledge contributions of others.
- Quick catch-up on what's been happening in your personal life.
- Prioritization: Are we clear about your goals for this quarter and priorities for those goals?
- Roadblocks: Is there anything in your way toward your goals? How can we work together to remove those roadblocks?

- Resources: Do you have everything you need to accomplish your goals? Do you need help?
- Feedback: Is there any positive or corrective feedback we have for each other?
- Travel/Time Off: What's coming up, do we know where we'll be?
- News/external: Anything going on beyond our department we should discuss?
- Professional/Personal Development
  - Any key issues in our lives that's impacting our performance?
  - Any training and development opportunities we want?
  - What did we learn since the last time we were together?
  - Revisit Position Alignment: balance of time, tasks you want to take on or reduce

APPENDIX 2

EXAMPLE POSITION ALIGNMENT

1·2·1 POSITION ALIGNMENT			
Position	*Director of Human Resources*	Manager	*CEO*

What are we counting on you to do? Break down the job into key buckets of responsibility.

1. CEO: leading and coordinating two companies, in-house "consultant," manage shared services.

   - Ensure hiring process is followed, provide metrics, make periodic improvements.
   - Generate and screen candidates, maintain ATS, administer assessments and compliance checks.
   - Manage interviewing process including training, improve the process, lead cultural interviewing team.
   - Manage involuntary termination w/management and legal, manage risk, prepare severance agreements as directed, support termination, conduct exit interview.
   - Develop and deliver HR-related training (required, leadership, soft skills), w/CPO, curate annual leader forum and manage regular forum meetings, lead team-led forum meetings.
   - Provide coaching and direct 360 feedback loops as requested by managers.

**Now:
20%
Goal:
25%**

2. Culture & Colleague Relations: Help make AI a great place to work.

- With CPO, define how we articulate our culture inside and outside for both AI and Bass.
- With management and support from CPO, resolve personnel issues through counseling and conflict resolution skills.
- Design employee survey, get feedback, execute and compile results, communicate results to colleagues.
- Manage biometric screening, compile and communicate results, design wellness programs.
- Plan celebrations (picnics, holiday parties, summer event, etc.).
- Facilitate Talent Review sessions by managing Talent Review schedule, providing data capturing tools, analyze results, encourage open dialogue.
- Work with the team to ensure that we have office space that meets our needs, fits our culture, connects us to the customer, and is fiscally responsible.
- Manage whole health strategy: design initiatives, measure progress, communicate improvements.

Now: 20%
Goal: 20%

3. Compensation & Benefits: Make sure people are paid correctly & administer benefits. - Ensure updates are processed in payroll on time, create total compensation statements. - Update payroll, assist with/back-up payroll processing, review payroll, and help resolve issues. - Provide salary survey data to management, conduct market pricing analysis; review market research on merit increase and review compensation planning with CEO/President, process bonuses. - Manage annual benefits renewal: provide census info, review options, and help communicate changes - Manage open enrollment: set timetable, provide employees with current benefit elections, update payroll, communicate elections to providers/employees, work w/provider to streamline enrollment. - Ensure all legal notices are issued, maintain summary of benefits for employees, manage benefits and 401(k) audits and Form 5500 filings, 401(k) admin contact/ investment committee.	**Now:** **20%** **Goal:** **25%**
4. General Admin/Compliance: Ensure we comply with regulations and keep us organized. - Stay current on HR rules, ensure legal notices are posted, keep AI in compliance with rules/laws. - Manage files, leave tracking, including FMLA, STD/ LTD, and other leaves of absence. - Handle accident investigations and prepare reports for insurance carrier as needed. - Update and communicate HR metrics, set new goals, celebrate improvements. - Maintain HR section of Intranet, manage monthly HR meetings, take notes, help create and review new policies; periodically issue new HR Handbook, respond to policy questions, interpret policies. - Lead HIPAA data security, ensure compliance, provide training.	**Now:** **20%** **Goal:** **15%**

5. Development: making me and the team better and getting us the careers we want. - Understand key needs of my team, identify holes, develop plan to fill needs, build bench strength, identify and develop high potential people, work with underperforming to improve. - Help my team understand more about their strengths. Help them get better and find the career they want. Develop rewards, plan and process compensation, support 1-2-1, recognize success. - Understand my strengths and weaknesses, identify my career desires, develop a plan to get better. Improve my leadership skills, support leadership forum, be a resource to other leaders. - Support and strengthen the culture, clearly understand and communicate purpose and culture.	**Now:** **10%** **Goal:** **20%**

USER MANUALS

Colleague User Manual Example 1

'm a "fixer" with the need to help people solve problems; I need to know if someone needs help to fix a problem or if they just need someone to talk things over with and vent.

I have an inquisitive personality; if there are any issues that arise, I need to know why and how to fix the problem. I have a tendency to ask many questions; mainly to gain knowledge and to learn from my mistakes or errors.

I need communication to thrive; I'm an extreme extrovert who enjoys meeting and talking with new people. I like to know about people and how they have gotten to where they are today. Please let me know if I ask too many questions or talk too much.

I'm a morning person and am more active in the morning than in the evening. I begin to trail off toward the end of the day—a quick cup of coffee typically perks me back up and I'm able to continue working.

Organization is key, everything has a place and should always be there. I'm a rule follower; I need to know the rules and regulations for everything.

I am extremely quick; if given a task I will finish it as soon as possible. This stems from my weakness of procrastination. If I let things linger, I will forget about them. When given a task, I like an outline of the overall vision for the project. It's easier for me to come up with an idea if I have this information provided.

My mind runs a mile a minute, and there are times when I may need to be reminded to focus. Also, if you catch me in the hallway and ask me for a favor, please be sure to follow up with an email. I have a tendency to forget things from one side of the building to the other. I typically remember to say, "Don't forget to send me an email."

Willing to learn and try new things or ideas. I absolutely love learning new trades and crafts. I have to be busy. I don't like downtime, unless I'm relaxing at home. I seek out new things to learn, which is why I learned woodworking and photography. I enjoy philanthropic activities—I like to volunteer/enjoy random acts of kindness.

Latest Version of User Manual

About Me

Things I really like:

- Equity and fairness. I like being able to design fairness into the organization, helping to decide what is right, looking out for others. I have a passion for creating a thriving workplace.
- Solving problems. I might get frustrated when wrestling with something complicated. Remind me to enjoy the process and that anything worth solving won't be really easy.
- Win-wins. I love when we can find a solution or action that benefits us in multiple ways (e.g., helping someone at work and home). I really don't like zero-sum games with big win and big loss.

My strengths are:

- Distilling information. I can cull through a lot of information quickly and distill it down to make it easier for people to digest. I like data better than hearsay, because it leads to better decisions.
- Communicating in writing. I'm better in written form than "live." I like to write and organize information so people are clear about what we're talking about and committing to.
- Focusing the issue. I find a lot of people and organizations start solving before defining the problem. I'm pretty good at organizing the pieces of the puzzle so we're all working on the problem together.

My areas for opportunity are:

- I can be impatient, so don't let me go on ahead if you're not ready for me to go. Help me realize that it usually takes time to do great things.
- I can be negative. Be enthusiastic, positive, and friendly. Help me see the bright side. It may not seem to be working, but stick with it, because it is. Be resilient.

Things I struggle with:

- Interruption. If you walk in and start talking to me, give me a minute to refocus on you. Scheduling time with me is even better. I like having time to prepare so I can better assist you.

Learning style:

- I like reading and learning the theory behind something before trying it. I want to see examples of how something is done. In school, I listened in every class and took great notes.

I am an Introvert/Extrovert:

- Introvert learning to live well in an extrovert role. I prefer smaller gatherings of close friends and really don't like large rooms full of people I don't know. I like speaking in front of groups when it's a subject I'm passionate about and prepared for.

Communication and Feedback

Best ways to communicate with me:

- Be prepared. Have an agenda. I like to get things done and I don't like to waste time. I work better when I clearly understand what we are working on and what we're trying to achieve.
- Prepare me. I will offer more value if you can give me information to digest ahead of time, especially data, background, questions, concerns, risks, recommendations.

Ways that I prefer to give feedback:

- I like to be able to give it directly and honestly in private. I will try to be specific and bring examples. I appreciate people who are open to critical feedback and appreciate the courage it takes to deliver it.

Ways I share feedback:

- I hate politics and game playing, so if I'm giving you feedback it's because I really care about you and the rest of the team and I'm trying to support a learning culture. Don't doubt my sincerity and care.

My communication style:

- I usually get down to business pretty quick. I should take a little more time to engage with you as a person, and I really like when people do so (within reason).

Structure

- In a meeting, have an agenda, even if I invited you. Have a plan and be prepared. We're spending valuable time to work on something together and not just meeting to hear ourselves talk.
- I work at odd times. If you get an email on Sunday morning, I don't expect you to answer it. If I need an answer now, I'll tell you. If you are unsure, ask what I want and when.

Support

- Things I value in a team are: Honest and respectful dialogue. People that take ownership and want to be part of the best solution. A team without drama, politics, games, ego. A team that takes responsibility, is accountable to clear metrics, is committed to high-quality work. Passion, positivity, energy, compassion. Learning from mistakes—after-action assessments and pre-action reports.

Environment:

- Optimal working environment: If working alone, when it's quiet or when I have noise-canceling headphones. Even better if I have a view or something to look at that is soothing. In a group, when we can get up or sit down whenever it suits you. When there is coffee, tea, or water. When there is a whiteboard and walk-up music.

Guiding Philosophies and/or Values:

- What I value most is: Family. Helping create an environment
  for people to thrive and team success. Service to others.
  Helping make the world a little bit better place. Trust, truth,
  heart, service, relentless.

Fun Facts about Me (Work or Personal)

- I love good food, good spirits, traveling, and exercise—
  preferably all tied together in a great trip.
- I don't do well with self-centered or greedy people. If you
  think about others first, you'll have a fan in me. If you're
  trying to make the world a better place, I'm with you.
- I am horrible with names and sometimes even forget my own.
  Please don't be offended if I forget yours (unless, of course,
  it's you, Honey). I remember the strangest stuff and forget the
  important things.

APPENDIX 4

EXAMPLE REFLECTION

1·2·1 POSITION REFLECTION			
Name	**CEO**	Date	**January 2019**

"STATE OF THE UNION" & SELF-APPRAISAL

Thumbnail: 2018 was a reinforcement of the power of Visioning. As we near 2020, we are able to look back and see many achievements. I don't see how that would have been possible without our work to create the vision together. For the first time, we're creating this Reflection, with achievements highlighted in each pillar of our vision. The progress we've made just in the last year is motivational and inspiring.	Overall 6

Highlights:
- #1 goal better products: monthly releases, record conversions, two new releases, quality improvements.
- #2 goal sales transition: new hires, new dashboard, retirement dates for key personnel.
  #3 goal regional growth: clearly defined regions and established detailed sales history within those definitions, identified issues & actions to make our drive to 2020.
- Brite Spot aware: named after colleague that found costs savings and implemented price increase that increased

recurring revenue by 10 percent and added 5 percent to gross margin.
- Accounting changes managed, great CFO hire, smooth 2019 planning process, clean audit.
- Installation completed below budget expense, on-time, high quality and SAFELY (0 lost time accidents).
- Culture: highest survey score + self-identification, solidifying 1-2-1, positive business webinar, Code of Conduct.

Lowlights:
- Key product released after survey season started, two new products late.
- Very difficult to find new talent leading to overworking folks we have and not enough time for planning.
- Continued challenges figuring out best organization and methods for driving regional growth.

Risks:
- Ability to execute on our regional growth strategy is hampered by tactical needs.
- Tight labor market in oil and gas and tech sector.
- Continued slide of oil prices affects budgets, general economic recession ahead, global political turmoil.
- Managing organizational changes, retirements, transitions, and effectiveness

Opportunities:
- New SaaS driving recurring—software growth will take its turn driving growth with better margins.
- ACLM mitigation growth and differentiated solution + patented hardware product.
- Strong backlog of home-run orders.

CEO	
- Led exploration into merger/acquisition with strategic partner. Ultimately successful in that we didn't do a deal that didn't fit. Fought against the tide to remain focused on synergies and cultural fit. Ultimately walked away from each other on good terms. - Continued march toward the culture we want &	25% --- Rating 7

more effective cross-company relationships. Service opportunities brewing under new leaders, more cross-selling and marketing, better balance of entrepreneur and centralization; however, this is taking too long to materialize. - Trying very hard to be a better, more positive, uplifting and complete leader.	
CFO - Overhaul of long-term incentive calculations and documentation—should have been done before, will be more important as we near end of our five-year term for this program. - Led move to new banker, support for loan application covering new HQ, negotiated incentives, worked with team on budget, contingencies, change orders. - Led hiring of new CFO, managed transition from departing VP. Completed analysis of Service group personnel costs to support billing rates. Managed transition of auditor, insurance relationships.	20% --- Rating 5
CPO - Talent review and compensation process improvements we began last year. Gathered data that supports efforts and presented to team. Presentation for all hands is with Culture Council for review. - Sharing CEO Reflection with leadership team helped train them and raised issues for discussion. Smaller follow up meetings provided more data on culture, areas for improvement, Reflection training. - Improved and shortened employee survey but did not launch it in all divisions. Completed 360 reviews for senior leadership.	25% --- Rating 7
General Counsel - Prosecuted new patent and had it issued in shorter time than we thought without having to give up significant claims. New trademark application approved.	20% --- Rating 7

- Worked >100 contracts—huge breadth and workload. Lots of progress on automated contract management system using Salesforce. Revised SaaS agreements to support new services.	

Development:
  - Finally took action on CFO after waiting too long. Would have been much farther ahead of where we are if we had made this move 1–2 years earlier. Good hire.
  - Managed a couple of key retirement discussions with heart and also with urgency. Managed risks and executed the transitions pretty smoothly.
	10%
	--- 	
	Rating
	5

APPENDIX 5

RECOGNITION

Ideas for expressing gratitude and recognizing colleagues. This list is from *The 24-Carrot Manager* (edited):

- Say thank you (and ask whether it is preferred in private or publicly before you do it).
- Send a letter of praise to spouse/family—praise in front of or to a spouse is powerful.
- Volunteer to do his least favorite task (and ask why it is his least favorite).
- Recognize special days (add birthdays and anniversaries to your calendar).
- Tickets to sports, movies, music, theater, etc. (find out what they love best or better yet what their spouse loves best; if you can afford season tickets, buy them and give away extras).
- Book by favorite author, subscription to favorite magazine (with a handwritten note).
- Organize a fun event, break in his or her honor (pizza for everyone to recognize . . .).
- Gift certificate to favorite store, restaurant (again,

find out what they love first).

- Buy lunch for him or her and 3–4 coworkers (and be sure they appreciate public recognition).
- Maid service, car wash, spa day, oil change, massage.
- Bring coffee, tea, favorite beverage.
- Time off, especially to do a favorite activity.
- Donate to their favorite charity.
- Have a gift box with variety of gift cards and let them choose the reward (you can use your company Amex to gather points and give the rewards to HR to distribute).
- Yearbook, scrapbook, home page with stories of recognition.
- Develop annual year-end award, lifetime achievement award, meaningful service awards.
- Come up with a fun traveling award or innovation award—or for a momentous accomplishment, name an achievement award after someone).

APPENDIX 6

VALUES

What does TRUTH mean to us?

Truth: We believe in honest and ethical behavior. We seek truth & face up to challenges. We do not hide failure or assign blame.

This means MORE than having integrity and ethical behavior. I think it is a given that we will not condone cheating and lying. Many companies have "integrity" or "honesty" in their values. A group of people without a basic sense of honor cannot possibly build anything positive. In our business, Truth means a lot more than just being trustworthy.

Truth means more to us. It means we face situations

> "Stand with anybody that stands right, stand with him while he is right and part with him when he goes wrong."
>
> – *Abraham Lincoln*, *speech in reply to Senator Stephen Douglas, Peoria, IL, October 16, 1854*

honestly. We want to know about problems. We don't sweep them under the rug or point fingers. You know that scene from *A Few Good Men* where Jack Nicholson's character says, "You can't handle the truth!" Well, we *CAN* handle the truth. We want it, we need it. I'm not all-knowing, all-seeing—nobody on our team is. It takes everyone being vigilant to identify issues and help us address them. It's hard to fix something if you don't know what's broken. So if you see a problem, point it out.

Blame and finger-pointing have no place here. If we're all going to be open and truthful about issues we find, we can't shoot the messenger. Solve the problem first. Figure out what went wrong and fix it without criticism. Make sure the issue doesn't repeat itself. Realize that nobody likes problems— don't expect happiness when you bring a problem to the table. You're a grown-up, though, so have the courage to raise the issue in the face of frowns and hand-wringing. Nobody should fear raising an issue. If you do, tell me. If you feel you were treated poorly because you raised an issue—you need to let me know immediately.

Don't wonder why or speculate. The truth is better than what you will find around the water cooler. Seek it out. I'll tell you anything that is not confidential. This is your business, too and you have a right to know what's going on. I love the quote above from Honest Abe Lincoln—I'm comfortable that we will always try to do right. If you think we're not doing right, don't assume we're wrong without knowing.

Truth means having authentic conversations. It's okay to disagree with anyone. It's okay to give critical feedback—the people we want here crave critical feedback because they are always looking to improve. I hate politics. Please, no kissing up around here. Tell the truth to anyone in the organization. Just be nice about it, and be open to it yourself. **Truth is the foundation of our values.** *As Mark Twain said, "Always do right. This will gratify some people and astonish the rest."*

More about what TRUST means to us

Trust: We trust employees to make meaningful decisions, and employees want the responsibility and freedom that comes with trust and accountability.

Trust is crucial; it's the foundation of all relationships. Trust is a prerequisite to ownership, because it strengthens self-confidence.

Before I joined AI, I worked for big corporations that didn't seem to trust their people. In my last job before AI, I was paid handsomely to analyze investment opportunities. This company would then pay an outside consulting agency even more money to present our analysis to management. That made us feel that we were not trustworthy and killed our ownership in the business.

> "Few things help an individual more than to place responsibility upon him and let him know that you trust him."
>
> *–Booker T. Washington*

When I took the opportunity at AI, I decided I wanted to put people in positions of responsibility, support them as best I could, and let them "run their business." This came naturally within HMI, because our owners operate the same way; I have incredible freedom and support to run AI without micromanagement and second-guessing. With that freedom comes a responsibility to do my best for the customers, employees, and shareholders—and not what's best for me personally.

I thought that if I could fill our business with people who loved the freedom that comes with responsibility—people who acted like owners and put the needs of others ahead of themselves—we could all be more productive, fulfilled, and happier.

I've told every employee, "Nobody knows your job better than you do. If I have to know your job as well as you, why are you here?" This is intended to create ownership, fulfillment, and productivity. If you just want to come into the office, get handed a to-do list, and blindly execute work, without thought or ownership, you should go work for a big company.

So we trust people to do their jobs and make decisions like owners. Because we are not micromanaging, we won't know what you are doing every minute of every day. Sometimes that gets interpreted as "management doesn't have a clue what I'm doing." The alternative however is that management knows all too well what you are doing. Which is worse?

This is a conscious choice. Because of Trust, our leadership will not know every detail, every issue, everything that is not working—by design, on purpose—because we choose instead to hire people who want to be trusted, who want responsibility, who want ownership. This means that our leadership is depending on you to know what's going on in your world and be comfortable raising issues or asking for help (see also Truth).

We believe people are inherently good, skilled adults who want to do their best.

Trust means risk. When you trust people, you are putting your fortunes in their hands. Sometimes that trust will be misplaced. It results in betrayal, disappointment, and hurt feelings. In business, it can result in lost sales, profits, or jobs.

It happens. We've had people steal from us, and I mean tens of thousands of dollars—not just taking home a few office supplies or padding an expense report. We've had people lie. We've had people make decisions that benefited them personally while hurting others. I spend a fair amount of time around other business leaders, and we're not alone; this happens everywhere. No matter how strong the culture or how big or small the business, people will do the darndest things.

When trust is betrayed, the initial reaction is usually to want to clamp down, kill freedom, and rein in trust. This is natural—when you get hurt, you don't want it to happen again. I think this is why a lot of big companies are so bureaucratic—there's just too many people to trust, so they move to a different model: people are inherently bad, so we need rules to protect ourselves.

We've faced that crossroads many times. Something bad happens and we want to say "That's it! No more fun, no more freedom—just do what I say!" Except that doesn't work either. It's degrading to everyone. And it's impossible to grow beyond a very small operation if one person calls all the shots. See Truth—even with a small group, one person can't be all-knowing and all-seeing. So we absorb those blows, suck it up, and are Relentless about trusting people.

So that's the deal here—that's the implicit agreement we have. The people we want here want responsibility, they want to be trusted, they want to act like owners. And we trust them to do so, we support them, and we help them succeed. We give them freedom to act. That means leadership needs to Trust people, and it means each person upholds that Trust. It also means that we need each and every person to be a guardian for that Trust and raise issues.

Too many times I've made the mistake of keeping someone around despite evidence that they were not a good fit for our culture because I felt they were critically important. I learned the hard way that nobody is that important. No matter how good you are or what "only you can do," if you do not live our values, we risk the entire culture by keeping you around. This especially applies to someone in a leadership position.

Trust is of course a two-way street. You want your manager and your coworkers to trust you. Think the best of your coworkers (including your leaders)—if you aren't satisfied with someone's performance, tell them, honestly and nicely, with respect. Trust that they will accept the feedback with grace, and return that trust when you give feedback. Don't ever "throw someone under the bus" and never, ever complain about a coworker to a customer.

A sure way to kill trust is to cast blame on someone else. It may be terribly tempting to "throw a coworker under the bus"—especially when faced with a problem that you didn't create and are getting heat about from a customer or our business. Don't give in to that temptation, especially in front of a customer. If trust is difficult to repair internally, it's that much more difficult externally.

So what do you do? Focus on the problem and not the blame. With the help of the other party, explore the issue. Clearly identify the problem, gather as many facts as possible, eliminate as much conjecture, emotion, and blame as possible. Come up with solutions. Test what you can—a short-term fix and, if necessary, a longer-term plan. Focusing on the problem does two important things: it moves the business forward and builds trust instead of eroding it.

Be accountable. Earn the trust. Make decisions like an owner, and we all benefit by having more opportunity, freedom, and control. Take responsibility for your actions. Don't be a victim—you have the power to improve any situation you don't like.

This is the importance and the great power in Trust. Greenleaf, in his 1988 essay "Servant: Retrospect & Prospect," said:

> The strongest, most productive institution over a long period of time is one in which, all other things being equal, there is the largest amount of voluntary action in support of the goals. The people do the right things at the right time to optimize total effectiveness because the goals are clear, they believe they are the right things to do, and they take the necessary actions without being instructed. No institution achieves this perfectly, but the one that achieves the most of this voluntary action will be judged strong.

APPENDIX 7

LEADERSHIP BASICS

"A boss creates fear; a leader, confidence. A boss fixes blame; a leader corrects mistakes. A boss knows all; a leader asks questions. A boss makes work drudgery; a leader makes it interesting. A boss is interested in himself or herself; a leader is interested in the group."[89]

"Leadership is endlessly challenging for many reasons including this one: leaders must be comfortable with seeming paradoxes, an ability to find the balance point between two opposing forces and impulses."[90]

"The art is trying to set the priorities and assemble a team so you wake up in the morning and actually have nothing to do."[91]

Leadership at AI is about more than knowing the Company's products, processes, history, values, and Employee Handbook. It's about more than making money. It's about more than "managing." And if you are a manager at AI, it sure as hell isn't about your title.

So what is it about? Well, this is a start of that answer—it's a summary of our "first level" of leadership training at AI.

These principles have been gained through some good books, the "school of hard knocks," our study of other leaders we admire, and our experiences with positive business.

Too often in the working world there isn't adequate training for leaders. Heck, even most people with an MBA don't have a lot of leadership skills needed in the office. Our hope is that we can instill years of hard learning into our leaders earlier and urge them to pass it along to all new leaders. We summarize important books to make it easier for our leaders to consume them, and we regularly circulate other educational materials and ideas to help our leaders continue to hone their skills.

And leadership at AI isn't for a select few—it isn't just for those who are organizationally responsible for others. It's intended for all—our vision is to have 100 percent of our colleagues trained in leadership and acting as leaders in our organization and in life. Our hope is that we have a culture where we are all responsible for each other, and that is the core of good leadership. To support that, we offer the same training that we provide our leaders for anyone who is interested in learning.

One of the important functions of our leadership forum is to discuss and debate leadership techniques— what works and what doesn't. The forum is a continuous learning opportunity, so every leader is encouraged to bring up new materials and influences to help the group improve. After all, we never know where our next great leadership lessons will come from.

- Servant leadership (*The Power of Servant-Leadership*

by Greenleaf): Put people's needs ahead of your own. Leadership is a responsibility to care for others, not a perk. Set clear goals, and firm fence line, then trust the team to figure it out. Help people become their best selves.

- Focus on strengths (*First, Break All the Rules* by Buckingham and Coffman): Look for the good in people and develop it. Help identify people's footpaths and superhighways. Be consistent, yet treat everyone as an individual. Define the right outcomes and stick to them. Look beyond job title.

- Motivate and care (*Nine Minutes on Monday* by Robbins, *Drive* by Pink): Autonomy, purpose, and mastery drive people more than money. Genuinely care about people and they will care too. Recognize, connect, bring joy and love to work, model good behavior, grow personally and professionally.

- Drive engagement (*Ownership Thinking* by Brad Hams): Good goal setting and metrics drive performance, learning, satisfaction, and well-being and avoid me-centricity, entitlement, and victims. Bring people "behind the curtain" to engage them in the "great game of business."

- Lead positively (*True to Yourself* by Albion, *Lift* by Quinn): Building a great business is destiny, not destination. Lead with doubt. Slow down, nourish the soil, reflect, have patience, avoid obsession with size, speed, and publicity. Demonstrate compassion, competence, and commitment.

These concepts are woven together with our values—one leads to another, that one ties to this one. This isn't just one book, one experience, or the flavor of the day. It's backed by research, data, and experience. It's not complete or perfect, but it is a good foundation to build on.

Our Historic Top Ten List

1. *The Power of Servant Leadership*, Robert Greenleaf
2. *Drive*, Daniel Pink
3. *First, Break All the Rules*, Marcus Buckingham and Curt Coffman
4. *Nine Minutes on Monday*, James Robbins
5. *Ownership Thinking*, Brad Hams
6. *True to Yourself*, Mark Albion
7. *Lift*, Ryan and Robert Quinn
8. *Managing Yourself*, Ari Weinzweig
9. *Daring Greatly*, Brené Brown
10. *How to Talk So Kids Will Listen and Listen So Kids Will Talk*, Adele Faber

The New Kids on the Block (for our leadership training):

11. *Conscious Capitalism,* John Mackey and Raj Sisodia
12. *Leaders Eat Last*, Simon Sinek
13. *Tribal Leadership*, Dave Logan, John King, and Halee Fischer-Wright
14. *The Ultimate Question*, Fred Reichheld
15. *Made to Stick*, Chip and Dan Heath
16. *Switch*, Chip and Dan Heath

17. *Profit from the Core*, Chris Zook and James Allen
18. *Give and Take*, Adam Grant
19. *Humble Inquiry*, Edgar Schein
20. *Fierce Conversations*, Susan Scott
21. *All You Have to Do Is Ask*, Wayne Baker

A note on *Conscious Capitalism*: While it is shown here as outside of the top ten, if I had to read only one book starting my journey, I think I would have liked to have started with this one. It is a great overview of why it's worth taking the harder and more impactful journey as a leader and why business is a force for good, and it covers a broad range of essential theory and practice for thriving organizations. It's not a deep dive into the foundational leadership practices. It is a wonderful book that I wish I had read before I started writing this one.

APPENDIX 8

VISION PILLARS

Example Drill Down

Company level pillar: We strengthen our culture and ensure it does not get diluted as we grow.

Describing what that means in more detail:

- We have best-in-class hiring, orientation, and training—our entire team is committed to finding and keeping great people. AI attracts talent because it is a great place to work.

- Departments, products lines, and "companies" have pride of team yet freely help other because it's the right thing to do. Internal competition is healthy, friendly, and respectful.

- Personal accountability exists with every employee, and blame is not part of our vocabulary. We openly acknowledge mistakes and learn from them.

- People openly and respectfully challenge ideas at all

levels to drive relentless improvement.

- All employees work together as owners to create a great business where people do the right thing without rules or authority to compel it, and people selflessly help each other.

Creating five pillars for the Culture pillar:

- Talent: Improved hiring and orientation that gets and keeps delightful talent (colleagues who delight coworkers, customers, and company).
- Training: Formalized, professional, practical development that makes our people better at home and at work.
- 1-2-1: Replace the traditional appraisal process with one that creates a positive partnership, alignment, and ownership.
- NPS: Deepening our connection to internal and external customer voices, through surveys, listening, and acting on feedback to improve.
- IAMAI/Bassitude: Strengthen, communicate, and protect our unique cultures; find the right balance between shared and individual AIT/Bass.

Driving specific quarterly actions to support each pillar (sample):

QTR	TALENT	TRAINING	121
Q415	Revise HO process New hiring packet Interview form training	Team $$ lunch & learn Replace Sam Law Leadership at AI.doc	Draft training schedule Finish 121 from leaders, Culture Council
Q116	New job description based on Position Alignment w/ADA categories	Detailed training plan Leadership Training#1 Finish Leadership Manual Does Forum do Leader#1?	Kick-off at All Hands, begin training – what does this training look like?
Q216	Basic interview training – including video, role play – offer this 2x per year	Improve Leader Training1 Financial Advisor training	50% of position alignments done; continue monthly working lunch sessions
Q316	Application on line Revise orientation – embed videos, refresh market videos	Visioning training – open to all, based on Zingerman's Business financial basics & dive into our financials (open to all esp leaders)	90% doing 121 meetings; continue monthly working lunch sections Quality check – survey all managers to see % done, test 10% of 121 for quality
Q416	Values questions – design specific questioning to get at values fit	Improve TS training – organize videos & materials for CP1 & CP2 on Sharepoint site	75% position, 100% of user manuals; help from marketing promoting success stories

ENDNOTES

Introduction

1. Brené Brown, *Daring Greatly* (New York: Avery, 2012), 185.

2. R. Wayne Boss, "Team Building and the Problem of Regression," *Journal of Applied Behavioral Science*, March 1, 1983.

3. Michael Parrish DuDell, "Get Your Business Book Published: Crown Publishing Group Editor Matt Inman Reveals How," *Forbes*, September 3, 2014.

4. Joe Iarocci, "Why Are There So Many Leadership Books? Here Are 5 Reasons," Cairnway. October 26, 2020, https://serveleadnow.com/why-are-there-so-many-leadership-books/.

Chapter 1: Compelling Purpose

5. As quoted in Daniel H. Pink, *Drive: The Surprising Truth about What Motivates Us* (New York: Riverhead Books, 2009), 8.

6. Ibid.

7. Ibid., 109.

8. Ibid., 131–45.

9. Robert E. Quinn and Anjan V. Thakor, "Imbue the Organization with a Higher Purpose," in Jane E. Dutton and Gretchen M. Spreitzer, eds., *How to Be a Positive Leader: Small Actions, Big Impact* (San Francisco: Berrett-Koehler, 2014), 100–112.

10. Ibid.

11. John Mackey and Rajendra Sisodia, *Conscious Capitalism* (Boston: Harvard Business Review Press, 2014), 59.

12. James Robbins, *Nine Minutes on Monday* (New York: McGraw-Hill, 2012), 139-40.

Chapter 2: Authentic Values

13. Simon Sinek, *Start with Why: How Great Leaders Inspire Everyone to Take Action* (New York: Penguin, 2009), 88.

14. Chip Heath and Dan Heath, *Made to Stick: Why Some Ideas Survive and Others Die* (New York: Random House, 2007), 56–57.

15. Ibid., 53.

16. Patrick Lencioni, *The Ideal Team Player: How to Recognize and Cultivate the Three Essential Virtues* (Hoboken, NJ: Jossey-Bass, 2016), 61.

17. Ibid., 157.

18. Ibid., 158.

19. Bill Burnett and Dave Evans, *Designing Your Life* (New York: Alfred A. Knopf, 2016), 38–39.

Chapter 3: Authentic Leadership

20. Robert K. Greenleaf, *The Servant as Leader*, Center for Applied Studies, 1970.

21. James Robbins, *Nine Minutes on Monday: The Quick and Easy Way to Go from Manager to Leader* (New York: McGraw-Hill, 2013), 44–45.

22. Fred Walumbwa, Bruce Avolio, William Gardner, Tara Wernsing, Suzanne Peterson, "Authentic Leadership: Development and Validation of a Theory-Based Measure," *Journal of Management* 34, no. 1 (February 2008): 89–126.

23. Edgar H. Schein, *Humble Inquiry: The Gentle Art of Asking Instead of Telling* (San Francisco: Barrett-Koehler, 2013), 5.

24. Mark Albion, *True to Yourself: Leading a Values-Based Business* (San Francisco: Barrett-Koehler, 2006), 17–18.

Chapter 4: Leadership Training

25. Simon Sinek, *Leaders Eat Last: Why Some Teams Pull Together and Other's Don't* (New York: Portfolio/Penguin, 2014), 16, 23.

26. Adele Faber and Elaine Mazlish, *How to Talk to Kids So They Will Listen and Listen So Kids Will Talk* (New York: Scribner, 1980), 1–2.

27. Noelle Pikus Pace, "What Are the 4 Simple Steps to Help Children and Youth Reach Their Goals?" Children and Youth Goals, https://childrenandyouthgoals.com/blog/2019/12/28/what-are-the-4-simple-steps-to-help-children-and-youth-reach-their-goals/.

Chapter 5: Visioning and Change

28. Bo Burlingham, "The Coolest Small Company in America," *Inc.*, January 2003.

29. Ari Weinzweig, *Zingerman's Guide to Good Leading Part 3, A Lapsed Anarchist's Approach to Managing Ourselves,* (Ann Arbor, MI: Zingerman's Press, 2013), 191–227.

30. Daniel H. Pink, *Drive: The Surprising Truth about What Motivates Us* (New York: Penguin, 2009), 107.

31. Weinzweig, *Zingerman's Guide to Good Leading Part 3*, 195.

32. Ibid., 197.

33. Ibid., 198.

34. Bill Burnett and Dave Evans, *Designing Your Life: How to Build a Well-Lived, Joyful Life* (New York: Alfred A. Knopf, 2016), 4–10.

35. Chip Heath and Dan Heath, *Switch: How to Change Things When Change Is Hard* (New York: Broadway Books, 2010).

36. Fred Reichheld, *The Ultimate Question: Driving Good Profits and True Growth* (Boston: Harvard Business School Press, 2006), 4.

37. Ibid., 142.

38. Ibid., 142.

39. Jane E. Dutton and Gretchen M. Spreitzer, editors, *How to Be a Positive Leader: Small Actions, Big Impact* (San Francisco: Barrett-Koehler, 2014), 11.

40. Omar S. Itani, Emily A. Goad, and Fernando Jaramillo, "Building Customer Relationships While Achieving Sales Performance Results: Is Listening the Holy Grail of Sales? *Journal of Business Research* 102 (September 2019): 120–30; Wilson Bastos and Sigal G. Barsade, "A New Look at Employee Happiness: How Employees' Perceptions of a Job as Offering Experiences versus Objects to Customers Influence Job-Related Happiness," *Organizational Behavior and Human Decision Processes* 161 (November 2020): 176–87; Guy Itzchakov, "Can Listening Training "Empower Service Employees? The Mediating Roles of Anxiety and Perspective-Taking," European Journal of Work and Organizational Psychology 29 (June 8, 2020): 938–52.

41. Ari Weinzweig, "Why ZXI? Part Two: More Learning from the Zingerman's Experience Indicator, Good Profits vs. Bad," Zingerman's (ZingTrain.com).

Chapter 8: Open-Book Fianance

42. Wayne Baker, "Understanding Positive Business: Open-Book Finance," Michigan Ross, January 8, 2015, https://michiganross.umich.edu/rtia-articles/positive-open-book-finance.

43. Brad Hams, *Ownership Thinking: How to End Entitlement and Create a Culture of Accountability, Purpose, and Profit* (New York: McGraw-Hill, 2012), 78.

Chapter 9: Compensation Process

44. Steven Scullen, Michael Mount, and Maynard Goff, "Understanding the Latent Structure of Job Performance Ratings," *Journal of Applied Psychology* 8, no. 6 (2000): 956–70.

45. Jena McGregor, "The Corporate Kabuki of Performance Appraisals, *The Washington Post*, February 14, 2013.

46. Clint Greenleaf, *Beyond the Piggy Bank: A Simple Plan for Raising Financially Capable Children* (Austin: Pigs and Bricks, 2020), 2.

47. Ibid., 6.

48. Ibid, 21.

49. Edgar Schein, *Humble Inquiry: The Gentle Art of Asking Instead of Telling* (San Francisco: Barrett-Koehler, 2013), 71.

Chapter 11: Second Jobs

50. James Robbins, *Nine Minutes on Monday* (New York: McGraw-Hill, 2013), 47.

Chapter 12: Gratitude

51. As quoted in Janice Kaplan, "It Pays to Give Thanks at the Office," *Wall Street Journal*, August 7, 2015.

52. The Boston Consulting Group and The Network, "Decoding Global Talent," October 2014, https://www.handelsblatt.com/downloads/13816620/2/global_talent.pdf?ticket=ST-6476821-XeETUCififzRjecOadeT-ap4.

53. Kaplan, "It Pays to Give Thanks at the Office."

54. Jane Dutton and Gretchen Spreitzer, *How to Be a Positive Leader: Small Actions, Big Impact* (San Francisco: Barrett-Koehler, 2014), 82.

55. James Robbins, *Nine Minutes on Monday* (New York: McGraw Hill. 2012), 96.

56. Robbins, *Nine Minutes on Monday*, 83.

57. Ibid., 91.

58. Ibid., 90.

59. Ibid., 90.

1-2-1 Process Introduction

60. R. Wayne Boss, "Team Building and the Problem of ReGression," *Journal of Applied Behavioral Science* (March 1, 1983): 70.

61. Lisa Barry, "Performance Management Is Broken," *Deloitte Insights*,

March 5, 2014. https://www2.deloitte.com/us/en/insights/focus/human-capital-trends/2014/hc-trends-2014-performance-management.html; Peter Cappelli and Anna Tavis, "The Performance Management Revolution," Harvard Business Review, October 2016. https://hbr.org/2016/10/the-performance-management-revolution.

62. R. Wayne Boss, "Team Building and the Problem of Regression," Journal of Applied Behavioral Science (March 1, 1983): 70.

63. "The Value of Training," IBM Training, 2014, https://www.ibm.com/training/pdfs/IBMTraining-TheValueofTraining.pdf.

64. "2018 Workplace Learning Report," LinkedIn Learning, https://learning.linkedin.com/content/dam/me/learning/en-us/pdfs/linkedin-learning-workplace-learning-report-2018.pdf.

65. Josh Bersin, "How to Build a High-Impact Learning Culture," June 14, 2010, https://joshbersin.com/2010/06/how-to-build-a-high-impact-learning-culture/.

66. Michael Nathanson, "Bringing Lifelong Learning to Your Organization," November 3, 2020, Chief Executive, https://chiefexecutive.net/bringing-lifelong-learning-to-your-organization/.

Chapter 13: 1-2-1 Check-ins

67. Edgar H. Schein, Humble Inquiry (San Francisco: Barrett-Koehler, 2013), 24.

68. R. Wayne Boss, "Team Building and the Problem of Regression," Journal of Applied Behavioral Science (March 1, 1983): 71.

69. Robert K. Greenleaf, The Power of Servant Leadership, ed. Larry C. Spears (San Francisco: Barrett-Koehler, 1998), 51.

70. R. Wayne Boss, "Team Building and the Problem of Regression," Journal of Applied Behavioral Science (March 1, 1983): 71.

Chapter 16: Goal Setting

71. Simon Sinek, "If You Don't Understand People, You Don't Understand Business," 99% Conference, October 9, 2011, https://www.youtube.com/watch?v=8grVwcPZnuw.

72. John Doerr, Measure What Matters: How Google, Bono, and the

Gates Foundation Rock the World with OKR (New York: Portfolio/Penguin, 2018), 7.

73. Ibid., 19.

74. Ibid., 77–78.

Chapter 17: Reflection

75. Theodore Roosevelt, from a speech delivered at the Sorbonne in Paris, April 23, 1910, available from the Theodore Roosevelt Center at Dickinson State University (https://www.theodorerooseveltcenter.org/Learn-About-TR/TR-Encyclopedia/Culture-and-Society/Man-in-the-Arena.aspx).

76. Brené Brown, *Daring Greatly* (New York: Avery, 2012), 2.

77. Peter Sheahan, as quoted in Brown, *Daring Greatly*, 65.

78. Edgar H. Schein, *Humble Inquiry* (San Francisco: Barrett-Koehler, 2013), 12.

Chapter 18: Development

79. Marcus Buckingham and Curt Coffman, *First, Break All the Rules: What the World's Greatest Managers Do Differently* (New York: Simon & Schuster, 2009), 164.

80. Jake Adams, "How Do I Talk to My Boss about Salary?" Wellspace, August 30, 2019, https://yourwellspace.com/how-do-i-talk-to-my-boss-about-my-salary/.

Conclusion

81. Alyson Shontell, "80% Hate Their Jobs—But Should You Choose a Passion or a Paycheck?" *Business Insider*, October 4, 2010, https://www.businessinsider.com/what-do-you-do-when-you-hate-your-job-2010-10.

82. John Mackey and Rajendra Sisodia, *Conscious Capitalism: Liberating the Heroic Spirit of Business* (Boston: Harvard Business Review Press, 2014), 26, 275–90.

83. Ibid., 24.

84. All Mankiw quotations are from N. Gregory Mankiw, "CEOs Are Qualified to Make Profits, Not Lead Society," *New York Times*, July 24, 2020, https://www.nytimes.com/2020/07/24/business/ceos-profits-shareholders.html.

85. Rosabeth Moss Kanter, *Think Outside the Building: How Advanced Leaders Can Change the World One Smart Innovation at a Time* (New York: Hachette, 2020), 30.

86. Ibid.

87. Simon Sinek, *Leaders Eat Last: Why Some Teams Pull Together and Others Don't* (New York: Portfolio/Penguin, 2014), 18–19.

88. Ibid., 214.

Appendix 7: Leadership Basics

89. Russell H. Ewing, 1885–1976.

90. Adam Bryant, *Quick and Nimble: Lessons from Leading CEOs on How to Create a Culture of Innovation* (New York: Henry Holt and Company, 2014), 243.

91. Ibid., 230.